SHARPEN YOUR SKILLS IN

*M*OTIVATING PEOPLE

TO PERFORM

SHARPEN YOUR SKILLS IN

*M*OTIVATING PEOPLE TO PERFORM

Trevor Bentley

The McGraw-Hill Companies

London · New York · St Louis · San Francisco · Auckland · Bogotá · Caracas
Lisbon · Madrid · Mexico · Milan · Montreal · New Delhi · Panama · Paris
San Juan · São Paulo · Singapore · Sydney · Tokyo · Toronto

Published by
McGraw-Hill Publishing Company
Shoppenhangers Road, Maidenhead, Berkshire, SL6 2QL, England
Telephone 01628 23432
Facsimile 01628 770224

British Library Cataloguing in Publication Data
Bentley, Trevor J.
   Sharpen your skills in motivating people to perform.
   (Manager's team development series)
   1. Employees – Training of   2. Employee motivation
   I. Title   II. Motivating people to perform
   658.3'14

   ISBN 0077090721

Library of Congress Cataloging-in-Publication Data
Bentley, Trevor J.
   Sharpen your skills in motivating people to perform / Trevor
Bentley.
      p. cm.
   Includes bibliographical references (p.).
   ISBN 0-07-709072-1
   1. Organizational learning. 2. Employee motivation.
3. Performance standards. I. Title.
   HD58.82.B46   1996
   658.3'14–dc20
                                       96-9742
                                          CIP

McGraw-Hill

A Division of The McGraw·Hill Companies

Some of the material in this book first appeared in *Bridging the Performance Gap*, written by Trevor Bentley, published by Gower, 1996.

12345 CUP 99876

Typeset by BookEns Ltd, Royston, Herts
Printed and bound in Great Britain at the University Press, Cambridge

Printed on permanent paper in compliance with ISO Standard 9706

CONTENTS

SERIES PREFACE

This series of books focuses on helping you to improve the performance of your team by providing a range of training and support materials. These materials can be used in a variety of ways to improve the knowledge and skills of your team.

Creating high performance is achieved by paying attention to three key elements:

- the skills, competencies of your people;
- the way these skills are applied;
- the support your people receive from you in applying their skills.

SKILL DEVELOPMENT

The books in this series will provide materials for the development of a range of skills on a subject-by-subject basis. Each book will provide information and exercises in manageable chunks which will be presented in a format that will allow you to choose the most appropriate way to deliver it to your staff. The contents will consist of all you need to guide your staff to a full understanding of the subject.

The books have been designed so that they can be used as individual workbooks.

There are at least four ways you could choose to guide the learning of your team:

- training sessions
- learning groups
- open learning
- experiential learning.

TRAINING SESSIONS

These can be run by bringing your people together and guiding them step by step through the materials, including the exercises. During these sessions you can invite your people to interact with you and the materials by asking questions and relating the materials to their current work. The materials will provide you with the detailed information you need to present the subject to your team.

LEARNING GROUPS

This approach involves dividing your team into small groups of two, three or four people and having a brief session with each group, introducing them to the materials. Each group then works through the materials and meets with you from time to time to assess progress and receive your guidance.

OPEN LEARNING

This approach invites your people to use the materials at their own speed and in their own way. This is a form of individual learning which can be managed by regular meetings between you and your team as individuals or in a group. The process is started by introducing the materials to your team and agreeing some 'learning outcomes' to be achieved.

EXPERIENTIAL LEARNING

This calls for you to invite your team to examine the materials using the exercises as a focus, and then to get them to relate what they are learning directly to real-life situations in the workplace. This experience of the learning is then shared and discussed by the team as a whole.

The books in the series have been designed to enable these four approaches to be used as well as other ways that you might think are more appropriate to your team's specific needs.

APPLYING SKILLS

Time spent developing skills can be wasted if people do not have the opportunity to practise these skills. It is important that you consider this aspect of performance before embarking on a particular programme. It is useful if you are able clearly to identify opportunities for practising skills and discuss these with your team. Providing opportunities for practising and further developing competency is part and parcel of the whole approach of this series.

PROVIDING SUPPORT

You will find more information on supporting your team's learning in Chapter 4.

Once people have acquired a new skill and have been provided with opportunities to apply it, they still need your support and coaching while they are experimenting with using the skill. This book, the opening book in this series, provides clear guidance on how to help people to develop their skills and then how to provide experience, practice and support as they use their skills.

Before starting work with your team on the materials in this book I suggest you do the following:

1. Review the materials yourself.
2. Plan the approach you are going to follow.
3. Discuss what you are planning with your team.
4. Agree some learning outcomes.
5. Indicate how you are going to support your team during the learning process.

The authors in the series have endeavoured to provide a range of materials that is comprehensive and will support you and your team. I hope that during this process you learn from and enjoy the experience.

Dr Trevor J. Bentley
Series Editor

ABOUT THE EDITORIAL PANEL

Susan Clayton is a leading contributor to the use and development of Gestalt philosophy and practice in organizations. Focusing on human processes, she enables managers and their staff to achieve business goals that depend on managing people. Her skill in raising awareness of how people relate to each other can forge supportive alliances and powerful cooperative relationships. Her approach includes helping people to manage blocks and difficulties in their contact with others, clearing the way for work and business relationships to move forward and grow.

Susan works with managers at all levels. Her interventions have aided groups in turmoil, managers needing to reach common agreement and individuals needing mentoring and coaching support. She helps organizations understand how to manage in a way that creates trust, respect and clarity in human relationships.

Mike Taylor is a consultant involved in the design, implementation and facilitation of personal and team development programmes within organizations. After graduating in 1987, he worked with two outdoor management training providers, both as a manager and tutor. His work has a strong focus on the use of experiential learning in developing managers, mainly within larger organizations.

He also works with groups and single individuals in running meetings and events that help teams and individuals explore working practices and approaches. More recently he has developed an interest in Gestalt as a way of understanding group processes. He is a member of the Association for Management Education and Development.

Dr Tony Voss is a counsellor, consultant and trainer. He originally trained as a chemist before working in environmental research developing seagoing computer systems and information technology, and later in the computer industry as a project manager, consultant and quality manager. Tony has a particular interest in enabling people to contribute fully and creatively to their endeavours, and sees this as benefiting individuals, their organizations and society at large. He is an Accredited Counsellor with the British Association for Counselling, and has also trained in Gestalt over four years.

Tony works with those wanting to develop their organizations and people, and those dealing with particular challenges in their working life. His clients also include those exploring the role of work in their life, as well as those with more personal issues.

*A*BOUT THE AUTHOR

Dr Trevor Bentley, Series Editor for this series, is a freelance organizational consultant, a facilitator and a writer. Prior to becoming a consultant and while working as a senior executive, Trevor carried out a major research project into decision making and organization structures for which he was awarded his PhD. Over the last 20 years he has had a wide range of experience working with organizations in over 20 countries. Trevor has trained for four years with Gestalt South West and attended Gestalt workshops in the UK and Europe. He now applies a Gestalt approach in his work.

Trevor has written 20 books and over 250 articles on business–related issues. His background includes careers as a management accountant, financial director, computer systems designer, a management services manager, a human–computer interface consultant, a trainer and a business manager. His current area of interest is in the application of a Gestalt approach to solving problems of organizational harmony. This includes culture change, performance management, team facilitation, executive coaching, mentoring and integrated supervision.

PART 1

HELPING PEOPLE TO LEARN

PART 1

For a number of years now there has been a move towards managers becoming more responsible for the development of 'their' people. This has been resisted by some managers who have taken the quite understandable stance that training is the responsibility of trainers and not managers.

It is, however, indisputable that the vast majority of the learning that people do is done 'on the job'. This may or may not be under the guidance of their managers, but it will happen through the natural desire we all have to learn.

If managers are able to learn how to assist this learning process it can considerably improve the speed and quality of learning and hence of the performance of the people concerned. Of course most managers are very busy people and they have the conflicting demands of spending time with their people or performing themselves. Perhaps one of the major problems facing managers today is this split between people and task orientation. There is no easy answer to this dilemma and managers will have to find their own way to balance these conflicting demands.

The four chapters in Part 1 of this book focus on how you can help people to learn – not by teaching or training them but by making sure that the working environment you create is conducive to learning and that you understand some of the basic ideas about learning.

This knowledge about learning will help you when using other books in this series to focus on specific topics about which your staff may need to learn.

CHAPTER 1

*T*HE WAYS PEOPLE LEARN

KEY LEARNING POINTS

- Understanding that people learn differently
- Appreciating that people have learning preferences
- Knowing about the four main learning styles
- Appreciating the implications of learning styles

PEOPLE LEARN DIFFERENTLY

Exercise – Learning preferences

Think for a moment about how you like to learn. Choose from the following list the approach that most closely matches the way that you think you learn the best. Then rank the list from 1–10 in order of the ways that you prefer to learn.

- Being thrown in at the deep end and sinking or swimming
- Being given information and asked to think about it
- Being shown what to do
- Being given the opportunity to have a go at doing something
- Being invited to explore some activity and to see what you get out of it

- Being presented with a problem to solve
- Being invited to play a game
- Learning on your own from written material
- Learning with a group of people by doing exercises together
- Being given information and then being tested on what you have learned

When you have completed this short exercise you might think that most other people would produce the same or a very similar result. You can test this by asking your staff or your colleagues to do the exercise and see what they come up with. If you do decide to test this idea that people learn differently, don't show them your outcome until they have had a go.

Unfortunately people are very rarely asked how they like to learn. In most schools pupils are grouped into classes and a single teaching approach is used for the whole group. This is also a common approach used in training courses. What happens in this group approach is that some people in the group will find the approach to their liking and they will learn from it, others will find the approach uninteresting and they will not learn from it.

It is believed that in most group learning situations 33% are left behind, 20% are ahead and bored, 47% are learning.

It is still not clear what makes people learn in different ways and many ideas have been put forward about inherited abilities and about experience. Perhaps the most sensible view is that we are born with certain innate abilities and that we acquire other abilities through experience. It is this combination that determines how we learn and we continue to adapt our approach throughout our lives.

Unfortunately for many people, the methods chosen to teach them in our education system tend to rely on the same approach of giving people information and then testing them on their ability to recall this information. Sometimes this is done to gauge how well people understand the information through testing their application of the knowledge. The idea that we need to cram our minds with information is ludicrous and few of us make use of the information we were required to learn at school and university.

The abilities to read and write and use computers are the basic essential pieces of learning that then enable us to access vast amounts of information.

WE ALL HAVE LEARNING PREFERENCES

If you did this exercise at the beginning of this chapter you probably identified your learning preferences. These preferences will be how you have developed your own learning style throughout all your years of education and experience. It is probable that your style works well for you and that when given the opportunity you will immediately, almost automatically, select your chosen approach. When you are not allowed to choose, you may try to adapt the approach being used to your preferred way and if this doesn't work you will probably become frustrated and struggle to learn or stop learning.

There are at least two ways in which people who are presenting you with a learning opportunity can approach this question of learning preference.

1. They can provide learning in a variety of ways that will feed a number of learning preferences.
2. They can discuss with you how you prefer to learn and then construct the learning opportunity accordingly.

The first of these two approaches is perhaps the most usual because it is easier to pre-prepare and set up than to tailor a learning opportunity to the needs of individuals. The second approach is the basis for most coaching that takes place because coaching is a personalized and individual approach, and this is true even when coaching a team.

See Chapter 11 for more on coaching

IMPLICATIONS OF LEARNING PREFERENCES

When we acknowledge that people prefer to learn in their own ways it affects the way that we present learning opportunities to them. Here is an example of a training programme that shows how we can allow for different preferences.

Scenario – Changing a car wheel

The requirement was to train a group of people to change a car wheel safely and successfully. The elements we included in the training were:

- a booklet explaining the process with diagrams and explanations;
- a demonstration of a wheel being changed;
- an opportunity to actually change a wheel with guidance;
- a video containing sequences of people doing it incorrectly from which learners had to identify the errors;
- a video of it being done correctly.

We tried using the materials in different sequences with different groups. Which sequence would best suit the way that you prefer to learn?

What we discovered was that the sequence which seemed to produce the best results was as follows:

- a video containing sequences of people doing it incorrectly from which learners had to identify the errors;
- a demonstration of a wheel being changed;
- an opportunity to actually change a wheel with guidance;
- a video of it being done correctly;
- a booklet explaining the process with diagrams and explanations.

Most people said that the booklet would be very useful to remind them of what they had learned from the programme.

So you can see that the four approaches need the same basic learning elements, but they are used in different ways with different emphasis. The basic elements are:

- information about the thing being learned to enable learners to conceptualize;
- examples of successful outcomes;
- information about how the successful outcomes are achieved;
- a range of exercises; and
- several examples of the thing being learned.

It is important to be able to offer learners this form of variety so that they can choose to follow their learning preferences. Perhaps it is worth emphasizing that variety is the spice of learning.

One of the big dangers that we face when helping people to learn is that we all have a tendency to project what we prefer to do on to other people. This means that if we prefer to learn in a certain way then we assume others would prefer this way as well. Sometimes they do but often they do not.

Cooperative learning is much more effective than competitive learning and more fun for learners.

When I am working with groups rather than produce a programme or agenda I ask the group how they would like to go about doing the learning. I offer them a variety of options for them to choose. I also invite them to cooperate with each other, helping each other to learn.

Learning groups that cooperate rather than compete and who can influence their approach to learning seem to progress quickly and enjoy their learning process.

ACTION LIST – THE WAYS THAT PEOPLE LEARN

1. Ask your team to complete the exercise at the start of this chapter.
2. Discuss the different learning preferences that your team have.
3. Discuss the scenario about changing a wheel and see which sequence they would prefer to follow as a group.
4. See if you can establish a 'team preference' for learning.

CONTINUOUS LEARNING

KEY LEARNING POINTS

- Understanding that we never stop learning
- Appreciating the difference between deliberate and accidental learning
- Understanding negative and positive learning
- Appreciating the need to maintain the continuous learning momentum

WE NEVER STOP LEARNING

Exercise – How we learn

To start you thinking about continuous learning, write down the last thing you remember learning. Now think about your own abilities and decide what percentage of them came from each of the following:

- formal training programmes
- on-the-job experience
- school/university
- life in general.

As human beings we are equipped to respond to and learn from our contact with the environment in which we live. When this natural learning process stops we die. We may not be aware of the extent of the learning that we do every day. Very few people at the end of each day stop and ask themselves, 'What have I learned today?' If we did then we would discover that every day we have learned something.

This continuous learning process happens because we are designed to interact with our environment and to take in vast amounts of information through our five senses. In other words, as we see, hear, taste, touch and smell, we learn. Each new or slightly different sensory experience is logged away in our minds and bodies. We are a constantly changing store-house of learning.

As this natural process operates we make choices about what we focus on and learn and what we learn in an unconscious way. As young children we are very focused on learning and we receive millions of signals and messages from our environment, including parents, teachers and friends.

Many of these messages become firmly embedded in our thinking and our approach to the world. Sometimes these messages are so strong and so frequently reinforced that they get 'programmed' into us. When we respond unthinkingly to these programmed messages we become prejudiced and dogmatic. We have, in other words, become stuck and we are blocking our continuing learning. This can happen in our work if we close our minds to new ways of doing things. Helping people to perform is not about installing your ideas in them, i.e. reprogramming them. It is about being open-minded and getting others to open their minds to the possibilities of continuous learning.

DELIBERATE AND ACCIDENTAL LEARNING

Deliberate learning can be described as being aware of what is happening and focusing on it. It involves making an effort. I imagine that as you are reading this you are aware of the impact the words are having and that you are focused on what this might mean for you. You are making an effort. This effort will not seem to be a strain if you are interested in what you are reading. You are in fact making a deliberate attempt to learn from what you are doing.

Training courses and training texts are an invitation for you to practise deliberate learning. There is an implied expectation that you will 'switch on' your 'learning process' and focus on what you are supposed to be learning. In actual fact our 'learning process' is always 'switched on' in stand-by mode and becomes activated when something new and interesting occurs.

We do not always have to be focused on what we are learning. Sometimes we learn accidentally. If we are open to whatever we are experiencing it is likely that we will learn from it even if we are unaware of the learning taking place.

The ability to be open to experience and thus to learn from it means that we have to accept the idea of continuous learning and to discount any notion that we have 'finished learning'. One of the problems with qualifications and competency levels is that once people have achieved them they tend to believe that their learning is over. I would suggest that it is just beginning.

THE LEARNING CURVE

The learning curve is a simple and well-known approach for depicting the stages of learning that learners go through when moving towards first becoming competent and then highly skilled. I show it in Figure 2.1 to give some indication of the emphasis that is placed on the deliberate and accidental, or unconscious stages of learning. When we start learning some new skill our approach is deliberate as we try to gain competency in the new skill. As we continue to practise and extend our experience, our learning becomes more unconscious. The more highly skilled we become the less conscious we are about our continuing learning.

The curve depicted will of course change in steepness

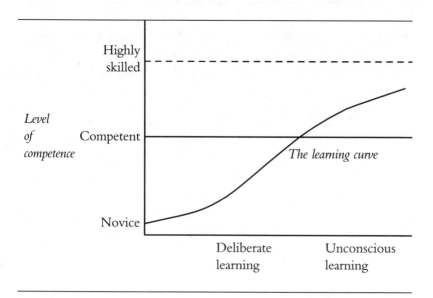

FIGURE 2.1: Continuous learning

and length depending upon the learners, the topic and the training approach used. However, the curve shown is representative of what is likely as a trend in all forms of learning.

The two primary stages of learning are usually preceded by a decision phase in which potential learners decide that for some reason they are ready to learn something. The reasons can be quite varied and can be both positive and negative, but for whatever reason learners will have made the decision to learn. When you are helping people to learn it is useful if you have some idea of what is motivating them to learn. It is not useful to assume that all learners are approaching the learning with a high level of positive motivation.

Check with your team by asking them the question: why are you learning this?

NEGATIVE AND POSITIVE LEARNING

It is perfectly feasible for people to have a strong negative motivation to learn. The one I remember from school days was to avoid punishment. The motivation to avoid some unpleasant outcome is an effective learning motivation and widely, if sometimes inappropriately, used to get people to learn.

Positive motivation is the drive to achieve or to gain some desirable outcome. This is also a powerful force that stimulates learning. Some people believe that positive motivation is more effective than negative motivation, but I have my doubts. The argument of which is best, carrot or stick, has been going on for a long time. I think both can be effective and that it boils down to preference, and I prefer to go along the positive motivation path.

'Skinner's box' became famous for studying the stimulus–response behaviour of animals. Skinner's ideas generated much controversy.

Frederic Skinner, the American psychologist, in his research came to the conclusion that if we were to keep rewarding a certain behaviour it would become a 'conditioned response' to the positive stimuli. The contrary was also true, that if a certain behaviour was given a negative (unpleasant) stimuli it would cease. However, when the negative stimuli is removed the old behaviour patterns return. This seems to indicate that learning with pleasant results (positive learning) stays, and learning with unpleasant results (negative learning) fades away.

When working with people to help them to perform it is useful if you can focus the learning around positive motivation to learn. This can be achieved by discussing the benefits of the learning with your staff.

MAINTAINING LEARNING DESIRE

People who achieve very high levels of performance, athletes for example, train continuously in order to reach their peak, to maintain themselves at their peak, and to expand their capabilities to new levels of achievement. What happens when they let up on their training, or stop altogether? They quickly fall below their previous performance levels.

The continuous learning process never stops (until we are dead), but it can slow down because people are not being exposed to new environmental stimuli. If every day at work is the same – meeting the same people, doing the same tasks – there is little if any new stimuli to encourage learning. Our powerful learning process remains in stand-by mode.

Of course learning is a process of choice and some people

choose to 'switch off'. This might be a result of the unchanging environment, or a choice to accept things as they are. Whatever the reason the process slows down and performance, far away from standing still, starts to decline.

Motivating your people to perform depends as much on understanding this continuous learning process as on any other factor. Maintaining the desire to learn is central to the aim we have for better performance. Part of meeting the challenge of maintaining learning desire is to foster an open-minded attitude to what is happening in the working environment and how people are responding.

ACTION LIST – CONTINUOUS LEARNING

1. Ask your staff what motivates them to learn.
2. Discuss with them whether or not they find their working environment one that motivates them to learn.
3. See if you and they can think of any way of improving the environment.
4. Talk about negative and positive motivation and ask them for examples, if any, in their current environment.
5. Ask your staff what causes them to 'switch off' their learning process.
6. Think about how, as a group, you could maintain the desire to learn.

CHAPTER 3

*T*HE LEARNING ENVIRONMENT

KEY LEARNING POINTS

- Being able to create a learning environment
- Being able to present the same things in different ways
- Being able to feed questioning minds
- Understanding the process of making learning choices

CREATING A LEARNING ENVIRONMENT

Providing opportunities to learn does not simply mean organizing training events, though this might be part of the process. Because people learn in different ways and are learning continuously, it is very supportive of their learning if you can continuously provide them with opportunities to learn. This can be achieved by creating a working environment which has a clear focus on 'learning and performing'.

I describe a learning environment as one in which:

People are encouraged to tackle tasks they know well in new ways and to have a go at tasks that are new to them. They are challenged and supported in exploring their own

capabilities in an environment where mistakes are seen as a basis of learning and not a cause for criticism.

The idea that mistakes are a basis for learning and not a reason for criticism is central to creating a good learning environment. Igor Stravinsky said:

I have learned throughout my life as a composer chiefly through my mistakes and pursuits of false assumptions not by my exposure to founts of wisdom and knowledge.

What was true for Stravinsky is true for each of us, but often we don't realize the importance of this self-evident truth. Each time I make a mistake I have an opportunity to learn, but this is lost if I am criticized because of the mistake.

See Chapter 8 for how to give non-critical feedback to your staff.

'Look what you've done now; good grief, don't you know any better? This is going to cause real problems.' This reaction to my mistake is more likely to elicit an apology and make me feel foolish than to help me to learn. It might also encourage me to avoid the experience in the future for fear of eliciting the same or even worse response.

'OK, so that is not exactly what we wanted, so let's look at what happened and what you did.' This reaction acknowledges the mistake but focuses on the opportunity that it presents to examine what happened and to learn from it. It demands no apology, it is not threatening, and doesn't carry blame.

I imagine that you might be thinking that this is all right up to a point, but what about the person who keeps making the same mistake? This is a good question, which I would change to 'what about the support the person is receiving to help them learn?' In my experience I have always found that people who repeatedly make mistakes have not received support and encouragement during their learning.

I recall one young woman who was having difficulty with a particular computer procedure. Her supervisor told me, 'She just doesn't understand. I must have explained it 10 times to her. It really frustrates me.' I spoke to the woman and then I showed her what to do on the machine. I asked her to watch me and then tell me what she saw. When we had finished she said, 'But it is so easy! No one showed me before.'

A good learning environment will also provide people with exciting, enjoyable, stimulating opportunities to learn through experience, with supportive guidance and access to information, demonstration, guided exercises and problems to solve. This means providing opportunities to learn the same things in different ways and so meet the needs of people who, as we know, learn differently.

LEARNING THE SAME THINGS IN DIFFERENT WAYS

In Chapter 1 I presented you with a scenario about changing a car wheel. In the scenario the same learning was offered in a variety of ways so that it would appeal to a wide range of learning styles. In creating a learning environment it is useful, as I have already said, to be able to provide learners with a choice of how they can learn. I believe that there are four principal ways in which this can be done.

David A. Kolb, in his book *Experiential Learning* (Kolb, 1984), describes a variety of 'learning styles' from which I have defined these four ways of learning.

- receiving information (hearing and reading it);
- observing what happens (seeing it);
- experiencing something (doing it);
- thinking about what happens (reflecting about it).

RECEIVING INFORMATION

It does not help people to learn if they are given information out of context of what they already understand. When information is given to people who haven't asked for it they might find it of general interest, but it is more likely to obscure any learning they might do.

Example – The ski instructor

'OK,' he said taking his ski pole and drawing a curve in the snow. 'This is the line of the turn, now here where I have marked the cross is the sweet point of the turn. As you approach the turn place your pole on the inside of the line at the sweet point and at the same time transfer your weight onto what becomes the downhill ski.'

To say I was confused would not be true. I understood the words the instructor had spoken but I was having some difficulty in converting them into any sensible message for my arms, legs, hips and knees. There was a distinct gap between what I had heard and what I could do. This feeling was confirmed as soon as I tried to do it.

The desire to give information as a primary step in the learning process is endemic in our education system and it is as ineffective as it is boring. The wonderful organism we call a human being works in a different way and this is true at all ages. As we experience something, if we want information we ask for it. We do this because we need to fill a gap between our current knowledge and the experience we are having. When we get the information the gap is filled and we can continue with the experience. If we are given information before the experience, we don't know which bit is relevant or useful to us, so we have to store it all in some way unrelated to our existing knowledge. If we don't soon find a use for it we will discard it.

So, instead of giving people information about what they are learning, we present them with exercises and problems to solve. As they do this they will need information and so we can give it to them in a way that is useful and so encourage learning. We do in fact feed questioning minds. Have you ever had to eat a meal when you weren't hungry? It's just the same feeling as being given information you don't want, and can't use.

OBSERVING WHAT HAPPENS

To demonstrate the value of observation I use some special wooden blocks which I hand out to the audience. They sit with the four wooden blocks in front of them. I then invite them to use the blocks to build a perfect pyramid. To help them I give them this description.

> 'You can build a pyramid from these four identical pieces of wood by placing them in pairs so that the rectangular sides are adjacent forming a square. Then take one pair and invert them through 180 degrees so that the square formed by the two rectangular sides sits on top of the same square on the other pair.'

Even if they hear me and understand my description most of them have great difficulty in doing it within the minute allocated. Even when I give them the information on a screen to read they still have difficulty. But after I have demonstrated it to them without any words, they can all do it within the allotted 20 seconds.

I imagine I can hear some of you saying, 'But that is OK with a visual and tactile problem, but what about intellectual problems that I can't demonstrate?' I have not yet met such a problem that couldn't be demonstrated through some physical analogy or metaphor.

Example – Inflation

In my managerial economics class we had to discuss inflation and its impact on the economy. Whether or not you have studied economics, if you think of the word 'inflation' and think of contexts other than economics I am sure you can come up with a suitable analogy or metaphor.

I used the idea of a balloon and with this simple device I demonstrated inflation and deflation, and overheating of the economy. You have to be creative to demonstrate. You have to innovate to demonstrate. It is easier to try to describe but harder for others to learn from what you describe.

EXPERIENCING SOMETHING

After a demonstration it is more effective to invite people to have a go than it is to try to explain what you think they saw. Of course it is important to make sure the environment in which the experiment takes place is protective of the learners.

It may even be a good idea to ask people to experiment before you demonstrate to them. In this way they will often be more attentive during the demonstration, or whatever other form the learning experience may be.

I was asked by a bank to look at the way junior managers learned to analyse balance sheets before agreeing to loans to small businesses. The course they were following had a section at the beginning which described the elements of the balance sheet. This was followed by a session on calculating balance sheet ratios, and then a session on interpreting the ratios. This is a typical example of giving people information before they know what it is for, or why they need it.

I suggested that we should change the programme and start with an example of a company balance sheet; we should ask them to analyse it and make a recommendation about lending. I suggested that by doing this the junior managers would discover what they did and didn't know and be more aware of the need for some analysis tools. By being more aware they would be more willing and able to learn about and use them. The course developers were adamant that it wouldn't work. So we did it anyway to see; that is, we experimented with it.

The first pilot programme ran and the outcome – and I hesitate to say it was what I expected – showed that, when presented with the problem, these resourceful young managers obtained and studied appropriate texts from the course materials and presented well-argued cases, including correctly worked ratio analysis. These were then discussed in a very energetic group session. In a much shorter space of time, with no lectures and with little guidance except to the materials, they had done a very good job of learning.

I believe that every piece of learning can be developed as an experiment, but it might take preparation to construct the appropriate environment. The more innovative the experiment the better.

THINKING ABOUT THINGS

In order to understand things we have to think about them. We have to put the information we gather via our senses into some context of past experience that we already understand.

When people learn to do something, such as make a telephone call or send a fax, they can do it without understanding what they are doing, in other words how the equipment actually works. They do not need this understanding in order to use the equipment but if they did need to understand, it would be necessary to obtain a lot more information and to think about it in the context of what they already know.

Sometimes when people are learning, although they may not need to understand what they are doing, they often want much more information than they are given so that they can gain 'some' understanding of what they are doing. To get this information they ask questions that they have formulated from thinking about what they would like to know. This process of thinking and questioning is a crucial learning process, and is one that people frequently make use of.

FEEDING QUESTIONING MINDS

Feeding questioning minds does not just mean providing written or spoken information. Language is one of the prime ways that we receive and process information, but it is not always the most appropriate way to learn. Words are symbols for the things we see, hear, taste, touch and smell. We can use them to describe abstract concepts that we cannot experience with our senses. But our senses are still the primary source of most of the information our organism processes from its experience in the world.

I believe that wherever possible we should make use of these powerful senses in learning, just as the young child does. This means creating sensory learning experiences whenever this can be done, and this is more often than you might expect.

Scenario – The bank's environment

The group of young people were together to learn about customer services. They all worked for the same bank. I had been asked to demonstrate to the trainers how a sensory experience could be built into the programme. I suggested to the group that they go to visit a branch of the bank as if they were a customer. 'I want you to concentrate on what you see, hear, touch, taste and smell.' When I said this they all laughed. One of them asked me why? I told them that I believed we were affected as much by what we sensed as what actually happens and what is said, but that I wanted them to experiment with this idea and then share their experiences.

The next day the group spent the morning doing what I had suggested. They assembled for lunch. The group were very talkative over lunch and keen to get back to the afternoon session. The feedback shocked both the group and the trainers. In summary what had been 'sensed' was a very noisy, unfriendly, untidy, dirty, smelly and 'tasteless' environment. Staff were sensed as artificial, pretentious and patronizing. When the young people had switched on their sensory perception they had discovered what they, even working in the environment, had previously put out of awareness.

In this scenario the questioning minds of the staff had been fed by all their senses and the resulting outcome was much more informative and a much more powerful learning experience.

MAKING LEARNING CHOICES

Training in the sense of 'drill' where people do things repetitively until it is embedded in the way they function is closer to Skinner's conditioning than to learning from choice.

I have encountered the idea, particularly among trainers, that training provides people with knowledge and skills. It does not. Training provides people with an opportunity to learn. It is an input to the learning process. If it is particularly good and appropriate training the outcome will be the desired learning. I say 'desired' because most training has an agenda and is designed to produce certain prescribed learning outcomes. But, and it is an important but, learners will still choose to learn only what they want to learn.

So training is not learning, nor is it an indicator that learning has happened just because people have undergone the training.

Training is the provision of effective meaningful learning opportunities. It includes providing courses, materials, experiences and practice in whatever is being learned. It is, or should be, designed to offer a variety of ways for participants to learn, and it should be clear about the expected outcomes.

The outcome of training is, or should be, learning and usually takes the form of:

■ enhanced knowledge about the subject;
■ some level of skill in the subject;
■ some desire to think differently (attitude change);
■ some desire to act differently (behaviour change).

Helping people to learn may involve the use of training facilities and resources when appropriate, but this can only support the learning that takes place in the workplace as people endeavour to use the new knowledge and skills they have obtained. It is this phase of the process in which you as a manager play such a vital role. It is vital that you encourage and support the learning of your people, and try to provide an environment conducive to learning. One of the keys to making the working/learning environment a powerful one is to provide people with choices, about when and how they learn.

ACTION LIST – PROVIDING OPPORTUNITIES TO LEARN

1. Talk to each of your staff and identify three aspects of their work in which they could do some learning.
2. Examine your working environment and decide how you could convert it into a learning environment.
3. Think of one way in which you could provide each member of your staff with a learning challenge.
4. In consultation with your staff, examine what choices they currently have about their learning.
5. Ask your staff each to think about two questions they would like to ask about their work.

CHAPTER 4

SUPPORTING THE LEARNING PROCESS

KEY LEARNING POINTS

- Being aware of the importance of encouragement
- Being able to help people to use what they have learned
- Knowing how to help people to be successful
- Being able to help people to gain competence

THE IMPORTANCE OF ENCOURAGEMENT

When people are learning they are often hesitant and unsure of their actions. It is likely that in the early stages of learning people will hold back from 'having a go' because they are concerned that they will not be able to do 'it' properly. This holding back from experiment and experience can considerably slow down their learning progress. If, at the exact moment of decision, you are able to encourage them to try 'it' and if you are able to show them that getting it wrong will not matter because you can easily put it right, you will be instrumental in helping them to learn.

Encouragement is a very powerful aspect of creating a

successful learning environment. It happens when you are able to show people that you have confidence in them and that you trust them to do the best they can. In this atmosphere you can enable them to learn quickly by attempting to use what they know or think they know. Converting knowledge into action is one of the most important aspects of learning. It is primarily through this process that we gain understanding and competence.

HELPING PEOPLE TO USE WHAT THEY HAVE LEARNED

When I am helping someone to learn, the hardest thing for me to do is to watch them struggle. The second hardest thing for me to do is to remember that what matters most is the effort they make and not the outcome. Unfortunately, in the modern commercial environment the focus is very much on outcomes and results. This can be a useful focus; however, in a learning environment if the focus is only on outcomes it will hold back the learning that people are prepared to 'risk' doing. The old adage that 'it is better to try and fail than never to have tried', has been changed to 'it is better not to try if you think you might fail'. The result of this is to slow down learning progress considerably.

If people are not encouraged to use the knowledge they have learned by using it in action they will gradually lose the knowledge.

After you have read the next paragraph, stop reading, put this book down and go and talk to your people. Ask them what knowledge they have that they would like to use in their work. Decide, with them, how you could set up these opportunities for them to 'try out' what they know. Encourage them to take risks and be prepared to support them while they are 'having a go'.

The knowledge you are gaining from this book about helping people to learn will be lost if you don't use it in a practical way. And don't do it once. Keep doing it. Practise what you are learning at every opportunity and through practice reinforce your learning.

Modelling continuous learning to your staff through being open and prepared to learn is an excellent way to encourage their learning.

Scenario – Closing the sale

David and Jenny are both members of a regional sales team. David is an experienced salesman and has been asked by the regional sales manager to help Jenny, who is struggling to close sales. David has little experience of helping people to learn, but he remembers how he learned from watching a more experienced salesman at work. He decides to take Jenny out with him for the day.

During the day Jenny is very attentive and asks David a lot of questions. Later she makes a lot of notes and tells David that she thinks she has a good idea about how she could close sales. David is pleased and takes Jenny out for another day. Towards the end of the day Jenny tells David that she would like to deal with the next customer. David agrees somewhat reluctantly. After the interview with the customer David points out to Jenny all the things she did wrong and why she didn't manage to close the sale. Jenny is upset and disillusioned and says to David, 'I feel as if I'm never going to get it right.'

When you read this scenario it may seem obvious to you that David did not really help Jenny. Take a few minutes and decide how you would have done it differently so that Jenny was enthused rather than disillusioned.

HELPING PEOPLE TO BE SUCCESSFUL

One of my favourite sayings is that 'failures are the stepping stones to success'. Of course this is only true if people have the courage to risk failing until they succeed. Not many of us have such courage and if the result of failure is criticism and ridicule, it is no wonder that we want to avoid failing.

See Chapter 8 for information on giving non-critical feedback.

It is possible to help people to learn and to help them to experience being successful at the same time as they are learning. This can be done by setting up learning opportunities at which people can succeed. Computer games are a very good example of people being offered different levels of difficulty; they can play the game by starting at a fairly easy level, at which they can succeed. The game designers know that if players cannot succeed early on, they will abandon the game.

The pleasure of success has three very important effects. First it boosts self-esteem; second it increases self-confidence; and third it encourages further development/learning. Failure has exactly the opposite impact for most people although for some people failure might work as a drive to 'prove' themselves.

When someone succeeds at some new task for the first time, the sense of personal achievement is considerable.

Scenario – Closing the sale 2

After Jenny's second day out with David, her boss Peter – who had heard from David that the day had not been a success – asked Jenny if he could help. They agreed to spend a day on the road together. Peter suggested that Jenny would talk to prospective customers and he would observe. Jenny was nervous at the first meeting. When they left the customer Peter asked Jenny how she felt. She told him that she felt awful because she hadn't made a sale. Peter told her that he doubted if he could have sold to that prospect and suggested several ways she might have handled it. Peter then suggested that Jenny should call on one of her existing customers. They did this and Jenny felt more confident and was able to take several orders.

As Jenny's confidence increased, Peter suggested that they call on some prospective customers. During all these visits Peter encouraged Jenny and gave her tips and ideas about what she could do. After a number of calls Jenny closed a good sale using one of Peter's tips. She was delighted. Peter complimented her and suggested they should call it a day. Jenny insisted that she wanted to make one more call which they did and she made another sale. After this day out with Peter, Jenny never looked back and became a very successful saleswoman.

Buy yourself a set of juggling balls and learn to juggle. You will enjoy discovering that you can juggle.

The joy we all have when we discover new abilities and new powers is a tremendous boost to our spirits to go on learning and developing our skills. And it doesn't stop when we reach competency in a particular skill.

HELPING PEOPLE TO GAIN COMPETENCE

In Chapter 2 we considered the idea of the learning curve, from novice to highly skilled. The first level to reach is to be competent. This means being able to perform a given task to a level that produces the desired outcomes. To achieve this level, people have to know:

- what they need to know;
- what they have to be able to do;
- what outcomes they are expected to produce.

Making these three aspects of competency crystal-clear is step one in helping people to achieve competency.

Step two is to help them first to gain the knowledge then to practise the task, showing them how to do it and guiding their experience. As you do this it is important to encourage them and to keep noticing how the outcomes are improving, even if such improvements are only slight.

Step three is keeping the focus on 'getting better'. It will take some people longer than others to achieve competency even when they have a variety of learning choices. This does not mean that they are less able than others, but only that they learn more slowly and, in some cases, more thoroughly and more effectively.

Once people have reached competency the target

changes to expanding their abilities to the highest level possible. This will mean providing challenging tasks and pushing them to their limits. Through these new opportunities for development, people will go beyond competency to high levels of performance. The limits to their growth are their own desires and determination, the support they get from you and the learning environment you create.

ACTION LIST – SUPPORTING THE LEARNING PROCESS

1. Talk to each member of your staff and see if there are any aspects of their work in which they are hesitating or holding back.
2. Consider when you last encouraged your people and think how you can do it now.
3. Look at what skills you have that you are not using in your work.
4. Take some time to look at the work that your people are doing and decide how you can help them to be successful.
5. Draw learning curves for yourself and each of your staff for your key job skills. Have you and they settled for being just above competent, or something better?

LEARNING IN THE WORKPLACE

The workplace is where people work; it is also where people learn. In fact it is possibly the most important place for people to learn. The difficulty is to embrace and encourage learning while the focus is on working and performing to the highest possible levels.

This seemingly contradictory situation can be created by paying attention to the natural processes of learning that take place whenever people do anything. Of course if you only see learning happening when some specific 'training' event is taking place then the link between work and learning is indeed tenuous.

In Part 2 we shall look at how the very processes of work can be harnessed as learning opportunities. The ability to recognize opportunities for people to learn from what they are doing is an important management skill. It will help you to recognize the difference between practice and experience and to be able to reconfigure work so that it supports the learning that people need to do. It will also help if you can learn to give staff feedback in a way that encourages and supports them.

CHAPTER 5

THE IMPORTANCE OF EXPERIENCE

KEY LEARNING POINTS

- Knowing the difference between experience and practice
- Recognizing the elements of experience
- Knowing that experience is learning not mastering
- Knowing that experience is broadening not deepening

THE DIFFERENCE BETWEEN EXPERIENCE AND PRACTICE

Think about areas of your work where you have had:

1. a lot of practice
2. a lot of experience

Prepare a summary of each of these and underline those in which you have both practice and experience. It is likely that these will be the areas where you are most competent.

Now let us consider the difference between practice and experience, because they are very different elements of our learning and development. They are sometimes confused with each other.

I recall that I once interviewed an applicant for a job. I asked her about her experience in designing training programmes. She answered that she had 15 years' experience of designing training programmes. When I looked more closely at what she had been doing, the reality was that she had one year's experience repeated 15 times. She was very *practised* at designing a particular kind of training programme for technical staff in a single company. Her *experience* was very limited.

Here are definitions for practice and experience.

Practice

The repeated performance of a task so that its future performance becomes embedded or ingrained in the performer's behaviour in order that it can be carried out time and time again in exactly the same way.

In its extreme form this is equivalent to Skinner's conditioning.

Experience

Participation in a wide variety of events and situations which results in the enhancement of learning and brings clarity of understanding to the application of existing knowledge and skills and/or the acquisition of new knowledge and skills.

Scenario – The golf story

Some years ago I decided to play golf. I bought some clubs. I had some lessons and I started to play with a friend who was a much more experienced golfer. After a few rounds at which I performed terribly I had some more lessons. My teacher suggested that I bought 100 second-hand golf balls and that I practised once a week hitting them down the practice field with my driver, then back up the field with an iron, then down the field with my pitching wedge. Then go on the putting green and putt until I was tired. He suggested that I was to do this on the Wednesday and to then play a round of golf on the Friday. I did this for a couple of weeks and started to play a reasonable round of golf.

For various reasons my practising became less and less until I stopped altogether. My experience playing different golf courses increased, as did my experience of a wide variety of rough areas, woodland, sand traps, streams, rivers and lakes bordering and strategically located on the various golf courses I played. My golf stayed about the same, terrible.

I don't like practising golf shots, it is boring and I don't have the drive to do it, so I have decided not to play golf. Because I don't have the motivation to practise I don't get pleasure out of my experience of playing golf. I am sure that if I were prepared to practise until I reached a certain satisfactory level of performance, I could then relax a little and enjoy my experience. I am simply not prepared to put in that much effort practising.

Giving up, as I did, happens to many people who do not receive support and encouragement to practise.

You can see from this example that practice is important and experience is important, but they are different.

RECOGNIZING THE ELEMENTS OF EXPERIENCE

A man has no ears for that for which experience has given him no access.

Nietzsche

Experience has four elements:

- something new that I have never met before;
- something that seems similar but is different;
- something that involves my participation;
- something that is challenging and involves some risk.

Facing the new requires people to call upon their reserves of knowledge and skills and to find some personal resource in order to deal with the situation. The new is often risky and challenging simply because it is new. What people often discover is that they can handle this new situation and in the process they tap into aspects of themselves that they may have been unaware they had.

The similar but different situation can be quite tricky because the initial response is to call on the previous experience, to which this one is similar, as a way of deciding what to do. Because this situation is different people find that they have to adapt the previous response in order to deal with the current event and so enhance their learning.

Participation is a crucial aspect of experience. To experience, people have to be involved in what is happening. Deciding what to do and how to do it is part of the learning that comes with experience. If people stand back and observe others they have not experienced the event. You have to be part of something to experience it.

Challenging and risky situations call for more than the application of knowledge and skill. The more experience people have had the more likely they are to be confident to attempt challenging and risky situations. What is called for is a willingness to 'have a go', and possibly to fail. If people are scared of failing, and if the environment is not tolerant of failure, people are unlikely to take the risk. This consequently limits their experience. It is very important for people to learn that they can survive failure.

See Chapter 6 about learning from our mistakes.

You can see that experience is very different from practice. So the expression 'she is a practised manager' means something quite different from 'she is an experienced manager'.

EXPERIENCE IS LEARNING NOT MASTERING

If I want to master something I have to focus my attention on what it is I want to master and I have to practise and practise until I have mastered it. In doing this my experience is limited to the task I want to master. I may seek experience in using the skill I am mastering, but this will be in a narrow area of the skill itself.

Experiencing, on the other hand, is a process of learning and extending my horizons beyond those I currently have. Experience involves me in testing what I know and can do. It requires me to explore the experience to discover things that I am not already aware of. It involves me in experimenting with new ways of doing things, new attitudes and new ideas. Experience is about change. It is about a willingness to adapt, to be different.

EXPERIENCE IS BROADENING NOT DEEPENING

Figure 5.1 is a simple and powerful way of looking at the difference between practice and experience. Both are important in helping people to learn and perform. We all need both to deepen and to broaden. However, there is a balance that has to be struck.

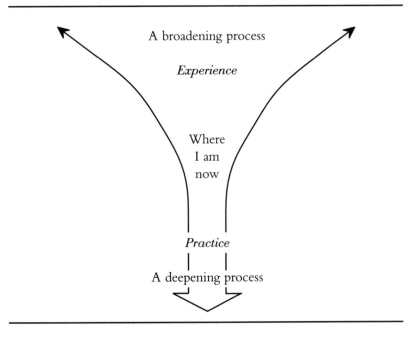

A broadening process

Experience

Where
I am
now

Practice

A deepening process

FIGURE 5.1: Practice vs experience

Practice alone will never equip anyone to deal with all the eventualities that are likely to arise in their lives, and experience without practice will probably be at best unenjoyable (as my golf was) and at worst quite frightening.

The deeper I go the more I limit myself, the narrower my perception becomes. The broader I am the more I open myself to opportunity and the wider I see. There is an old proverb which states that 'the jack of all trades is the master of none'. But the modern world is changing and what is perhaps more relevant today than mastering a single skill is the ability to be able to adapt and adjust as things change.

Perhaps the skill of 'adaptability' is one that we all need to develop.

Helping people to perform means encouraging people to be open to change, in order to experience more and to be willing to explore their own potential.

ACTION LIST – THE IMPORTANCE OF EXPERIENCE

1. Examine the work of each of your staff and decide where they might benefit from:
   (a) practice,
   (b) experience.
2. Talk to each of your people and identify an experience they could be offered that is new, challenging and risky.
3. Write a list of those things at which you consider yourself to be a master.
4. Using the diagram (Figure 5.1), talk to each of your staff and see if you can identify aspects of their work that need:
   (a) broadening,
   (b) deepening.

CHAPTER 6

PRACTISING –
A CHANCE TO MAKE
MISTAKES

KEY LEARNING POINTS

- Understanding why practice makes perfect
- Appreciating that practice can also make narrow
- Understanding that practice is 'learning from mistakes' in action
- Being able to remove the fear of failure

PRACTICE MAKES PERFECT

It has long been held as a basic truth that the more we practise something the better we get. But whether we learn from practice or practise what we learn is quite another question.

I have three juggling balls and from time to time I juggle them for a few minutes. Whenever I pick them up I can start juggling immediately. When I first learned to juggle I was shown how to do it, that is, someone demonstrated the skill to me. I was then encouraged to juggle two balls with one hand and then to introduce the third ball. I gradually learned how to juggle. Once I had the idea of what to do and my hands and eyes became coordinated I could practise. By practising I can now juggle three balls. No matter how much more I practise it will not help me to juggle four balls until I learn how to do it.

In order to practise, people have to keep repeating the task over and over again. Each time they do this their minds and bodies make very tiny adjustments, or corrections, so that they slowly get better at what they are doing. Eventually the task becomes ingrained in their muscles and embedded in their minds. They can do it automatically.

> This process is known as 'organismic learning' as it involves our whole organism in the process.

So, in the sense of being able to repeat a task to a high level of competence, practice does make perfect. By repeating the task time and time again, or drilling ourselves, we can become conditioned to perform instinctively. The gunfighters of the American West became lightning fast at the draw and accurate by this process of continuous drill. It is a method used for training soldiers to respond automatically and to a high level of competence under extreme conditions.

> We can see from this how important Skinner's work has been in the process of conditioning.

But change the conditions, and what happens? In my juggling, if I were to change the soft balls for crystal goblets or knives I am pretty sure I wouldn't be able to juggle them. I could learn if the conditions were to be accepting of my mistakes, in other words if it didn't matter how many goblets I broke, or if I could protect my hands from being cut by the knives. Then I could make the corrections that each mistake would signal were necessary to me.

So practice is really the art of making mistakes. Each mistake feeds a signal back to the body and the mind and a small correction is made for the next attempt. If you can recall learning to ride a bicycle, the very wobbly first attempt became honed through the corrections signalled by many mistakes to a confident smooth ride.

If people are expected to practise in an environment that is not tolerant of mistakes it will be very difficult for them to practise with the freedom necessary to increase their skills rapidly. The fear of failure stops people from practising.

Practice can also be boring and so people need to be encouraged and motivated to practise. I gave up golf because of my lack of interest and my boredom with practising, and I had little encouragement from anyone else to help me to continue.

PRACTICE MAKES NARROW

This is not a proverb, but it should be. If people practise to the point that they become highly conditioned to a particular skill it can narrow their outlook on life and their opportunities.

Highly practised people with a limited experience can face considerable personal difficulties if their skill becomes obsolete. They find that they have nothing to offer any more. Their self-esteem can be severely damaged and they can become depressed and even suicidal. This has been a common scenario for many skilled workers over the last few decades as working 'practices' have changed and new skills have been needed. Miners with 35 years of practice at the same pit face a very difficult time when the pit closes. Even the financial compensation for the loss of opportunity to use their considerable skill is hardly more than a sop to someone who feels obsolete.

Sometimes we go so deep into a particular skill that we become stuck. We may well be masters of our particular trade, but we may also find that we become unwilling to do anything else. In other words we continue to practise but we stop learning. When this happens, we become unable to adapt and resistant to change. When the goal posts are moved we can no longer adjust to score a goal and we get dropped from the team.

For many people, becoming stuck is something that happens without them being aware. They don't feel stuck until something changes.

Consider the people who work for you and decide if you have any people who are stuck. If so then you may need to focus on this issue with them and at least try to establish if they want to do anything about it.

LEARNING FROM MISTAKES

Mistakes are an opportunity to learn. In Chapter 3 I pointed out that part of a good learning environment is the recognition that mistakes are an opportunity to learn. Of course this is only true if the people making the mistakes are aware of the learning they can do, and if the manager involved recognizes the mistake as an opportunity to learn rather than as a nuisance or as a reason for criticism and discipline.

Think for a moment about how you react to negative criticism you might receive about something for which you have done your best. See which of the following reactions most closely matches your own reaction:

- disappointment and determination to do better;
- irritation with your manager;
- irritation and a reluctance to do it again;
- anger and a defensive retort;
- increased negative motivation to 'get it right', i.e. to avoid future criticism;
- understanding and apologies;
- understanding and wanting to learn from the criticism;
- increased positive motivation to please your manager;
- silent determination to 'get it right' to show your manager;
- being upset and determined to avoid the situation in the future.

The response of someone who is criticized in a negative way is rarely positive. But what about 'constructive criticism'? This is a contradiction in terms. The opposite of negative criticism is positive feedback which involves no criticism at all. I devote Chapter 8 entirely to the topic of feedback because it is so important. For the moment, in order to learn from mistakes we have to have an environment that makes it possible, and this means **no criticism**.

Some people feel that learning to 'take' criticism is part of growing up. This may be true but it always remains difficult, and it is not necessary, for anyone to have to 'take' criticism.

So how can we help people to learn from mistakes? Well, the first thing we can do is to think of mistakes as 'miss-takes'. In the film industry even the very best and most skilled actors have many 'takes' in order to get a sequence just right. There is no criticism. Instead there is encouragement and suggestion from the director to which the best actors respond and learn from; this is how they become the best.

A 'miss-take', then, is a chance to learn, but learning will not happen unless the person making the 'miss-take' is able to see what might be changed in order to make the next attempt a 'good-take'.

Every time that people for whose work you are responsible make a 'miss-take', you might find it helpful to do four things:

- acknowledge the 'miss-take' non-critically (see Chapter 8);
- find out from them what happened (awareness);
- show them what to do;
- ask them to demonstrate that they can do it.

Awareness of what happens is crucial to making changes in carrying out the task, and it is the performer's awareness which needs to be focused on. Just telling people what you think is happening is not enough unless they know what they are doing and how they could change.

Stay with this cycle of activity until they are happy that they can do it in the required way. This cycle of activity is in fact 'guided practice' in action.

Scenario – The four-colour print run

Dave Thomas, production manager, had explained to Steve that he wanted him to practise what he had learned on the training course for operating the four-colour printer. Steve had set up the machine and carried out a trial run. The colour registration was very poor.

Dave OK Steve, you can see as well as me that the colour registration is not what we expect.

Steve You're right, it's terrible.

Dave So tell me what you did.

Steve Well, I set the plates on the rollers and did a test

> run. The colours seemed all wrong so I tried adjusting each plate in turn, and it hasn't got any better.
>
> **Dave** Did you check that you had the right plates on the right rollers?
>
> **Steve** No, I haven't. Do you think that's the problem?
>
> **Dave** OK, why don't you check now and we'll see.
>
> Steve checked the plates and found that he had put two of them on the wrong colour rollers. Dave suggested he corrected it and have another go.
>
> **Steve** Look Dave, I've got it almost right.
>
> **Dave** Yes, that's looking much better. Why not try adjusting the magenta plate?
>
> **Steve** Right, I will.
>
> Steve did what Dave suggested and he was delighted when he produced a copy he had printed with a near-perfect registration.
>
> **Steve** How did you know which plate it was?
>
> **Dave** Well, when you get a red edge on the frame like you had, it is usually the magenta plate that needs adjusting.
>
> **Steve** Thanks Dave, that's really helpful.
>
> **Dave** OK Steve, now I want you to get another job and have another go.

This process of following the four steps in the cycle leads to effective learning and positively encourages people to practise what they are learning without the fear of making mistakes. In fact, in this scenario Dave never treated what Steve did as a mistake, but only as 'miss-takes'.

REMOVING THE FEAR OF FAILURE

In the minds of many people, mistakes are synonymous with failure, and failure means criticism, ridicule and even

Most of us learn about mistakes and failure at a very early age and this is something that is continually reinforced in the education system, i.e. marks out of 10, grades, etc.

punishment. These result in people developing a poor opinion of themselves and losing confidence. There is little wonder that many people fear failure. To remove this fear people need to be able to learn in an atmosphere that completely rejects any idea of failure.

For this to happen:

- mistakes are treated as 'miss-takes';
- mistakes are never criticized;
- mistakes are never punished;
- mistakes are seen as a chance to learn;
- mistakes are seen as stepping-stones to success.

In this way mistakes are not seen as failure, but as a positive result of practise towards becoming successful.

ACTION LIST – PRACTISING: A CHANCE TO MAKE MISTAKES

1. Buy three juggling balls and learn to juggle. During this process, experience how you learn from your mistakes.
2. If you can identify those people working for you who have become narrow in experience, explore with them how you can help them to broaden themselves.
3. Examine your attitudes to giving and receiving criticism.
4. Consider how you can produce a statement for your work team which removes the fear of failure and encourages them to practise their skills.

CHAPTER 7

PROVIDING OPPORTUNITIES AND CHALLENGES

KEY LEARNING POINTS

- Understanding what happens when we wait for opportunities to arise
- Knowing how to look for opportunities
- Being able to create opportunities
- Being able to challenge people appropriately

Scenario – Putting out fires

Joyce has just returned from a training programme on customer services which included training for identifying sales opportunities. Her boss, Doreen, has told Joyce that as soon as they are less busy she will help her to practise her new skills.

A few days later two of the more senior staff have to take sick leave. Doreen speaks to Joyce.

Doreen   This is your chance to practise your new skills on identifying sales.

Joyce   I'm willing to have a go, but I'm nervous. You'll have to help me.

Doreen   Yes, of course I will.

The day starts easily enough and Joyce's confidence is growing. Then around midday the branch gets very busy. Joyce begins to get flustered. She takes the first chance she can to speak to Doreen.

Joyce   Excuse me, Doreen, but I'm getting really confused; could you show me what to do?

Doreen   Not right now – you can see I'm busy and we're short-staffed as you know. I'll come over as soon as I can.

There is a lull in the middle of the afternoon and Doreen goes over to see Joyce, who by now is ready to burst into tears.

Doreen   Well, you seem to be coping OK.

Joyce   It's been awful. I don't know whether I'm coming or going. The customers have mostly been very understanding but I feel terrible. I seem to have forgotten all that I'm supposed to have learned.

Doreen   OK, it doesn't seem to have been a very good idea to launch you in at the deep end. You take a break and I'll fill in for you.

WAITING FOR OPPORTUNITIES TO ARISE

In this scenario the 'opportunity' created by the two staff being off sick is not an appropriate moment for Joyce to be invited to practise and gain experience. What do you think the outcome of this approach will be for Joyce?

In many work situations the pressure to perform seems to prevent any genuine opportunities for learning.

Waiting for opportunities to arise for people to gain experience is not usually the most effective approach. This is because:

- When the opportunity does arise there is no warning and no time to prepare.
- Putting out fires is not usually a good time to practise or gain experience in using new skills.
- The infrequency with which opportunities occur mean that the experience is spasmodic and there is hardly time to consolidate the learning.

Another significant problem in waiting for opportunities to arise is that they pass before they can be used as learning opportunities. This can happen because the situation is dealt with by a more experienced person on the basis that 'it is easier to do it myself than to show a trainee what to do'. It is also possible that we can wait a long time for an appropriate opportunity, and sometimes they just do not occur.

LOOKING FOR OPPORTUNITIES

At this moment, do you know what opportunities your staff need in order to enhance their learning and their experience? Arrange to talk to them about the opportunities that they think might be appropriate. It is probable that you won't be able to provide for all these needs and some of them might even surprise you.

When you have done this, list the opportunities that your staff want and start to think about how you could start to 'look out' for likely events. It might be possible for you to look at your own workload and to see how much of this might consist of opportunities for your staff.

This 'looking for opportunities' means that you can increase your awareness of what might be possible. Your people will probably help you in looking for appropriate opportunities and you could encourage them to make suggestions to you.

The workplace is usually, but not always, a fruitful source of opportunities for people to learn, practise and gain experience, but sometimes it is useful to look outside the confines of work for opportunities. This broadening of the possible source of opportunities is both practical and exciting, and makes a useful link between work and life. All too often, what happens in the workplace and what happens outside are kept very separate, but it doesn't have to be like that. All kinds of skills needed in the workplace can be practised and experience can be extended in the lives that people have outside the organization.

If you and your staff seek out opportunities wherever they may be, then it is likely that plenty will be found. I believe strongly that it is up to you and each member of your staff to be on the look-out for suitable opportunities.

CREATING OPPORTUNITIES

One of the main roles of training is the creation of learning opportunities. Frequently this is done away from the workplace both to avoid disrupting the work and to ensure learners can concentrate on their learning, i.e. that they are not distracted by the moment-to-moment demands of the job. There is also the added advantage of meeting other people at the same or similar stage of learning.

However, learning opportunities can be created in the workplace, not necessarily to replace training but to complement it. The first place to look to create learning opportunities is the work itself. In Chapter 4 I provided a scenario about 'closing the sale' which used the workplace as a very powerful learning opportunity for Jenny.

The approach to creating this kind of learning opportunity is to follow four steps:

1. Decide with the person concerned what needs to be learned, practised and/or experienced. These are the **learning outcomes**.
2. Decide the simplest way that this can be done.
3. You will need to agree what part you are going to play in the activity and whether other staff will be involved.
4. Finally, together with the person concerned, you will need to set up the learning activity.

Scenario – Identifying customer needs

In the first scenario in this chapter, Doreen attempted to help Joyce but the situation she chose was not appropriate. After some thinking and discussion with Joyce, Doreen has decided to set up a learning opportunity. They have agreed to start an hour early in the morning. Doreen has asked some staff from a nearby branch to help by acting as customers with certain needs. The idea is for them to come to the branch and be seen by Joyce who will try to identify their needs. After this exercise Joyce and Doreen and the pseudo-customers will meet to discuss their experiences.

This form of creative activity is perfectly possible in most working situations; of course you know your own situation and can decide what is and is not possible. I would encourage you to search for as many ways of helping your people to learn as you can, because this is the road to high performance.

CHALLENGING YOUR PEOPLE

Throwing people in at the deep end is one way of challenging them. It is also a good way of 'killing them off', metaphorically speaking of course. I want to look at three other, less risky and more supportive ways of challenging your people. These are:

■ keeping them on their toes;

- inviting people to grow;
- sharing your job.

KEEPING THEM ON THEIR TOES

I am not sure if this saying comes from ballet, or whether it simply means standing on tiptoe to reach for something. Either way you can imagine how challenging it would be to stay a long time on your toes. The saying has come to mean keeping people constantly focused on what they are doing and getting them to reach beyond themselves.

The way I interpret this in terms of motivating people to perform is to be aware of when people are able to perform comfortably and to find additional tasks that will stretch them further. This is one way that people rise from the plateau of competency to the summit of high performance.

You may want to refer to Chapter 2 to remind yourself of the 'learning curve'.

INVITING PEOPLE TO GROW

Here are four questions that you could ask your staff that are all invitations to grow.

- Would you like a change from what you are doing?
- Are you interested in doing ...?
- Would you like to help me with ...?
- There are several additional tasks I would like you to do; which would you prefer?

Stop for a moment and imagine how you would feel if your manager were to ask you one of these questions. You might feel excited, apprehensive, suspicious – it all depends on the relationship you have with your manager – but I bet you would be stirred in some way.

If the questions contain some interesting and stretching activity they become a form of confirmation of the person's ability. Think about the members of your staff and see if you can find a way of inviting each of them to grow.

This is not another approach to delegation. It is literally a temporary sharing so that people can learn.

SHARING YOUR JOB

It is probable that there are aspects of your job that would make excellent learning opportunities for your staff. If you invited people to take on part of what you do, you would need to provide support for them while they are doing it. Here are some thoughts for you:

- Invite a member of staff to do your job for one day.
- Invite one of your staff to accompany you to one of the meetings you have to attend.
- Invite someone to attend a meeting in your place.
- Select a particular task you have to do and invite one of your staff to do it.

You can probably think of other things you could do to give your staff challenging opportunities by sharing your job. If you take this approach it is helpful if you do the following:

- brief the person concerned;
- be available to help them;
- encourage them;
- don't criticize them if they have a 'miss-take'.

Perhaps the overall key to providing work-based learning opportunities is to use the real activities that take place, or create simulations which are as close to reality as possible. Doing this with your help and support can lead to significant increases in competence, confidence and performance.

ACTION LIST – PROVIDING OPPORTUNITIES AND CHALLENGES

1. Talk to each member of your team and decide upon a learning opportunity that would be valuable to that person.
2. Consider each member of your staff and think about a way in which you could provide him or her with a challenge.
3. Look at your own job and see which aspects of it might provide excellent learning opportunities for your staff.
4. Prepare a schedule of learning opportunities and challenges and discuss them with your staff, asking them to be on the look out for suitable situations.
5. Start providing learning opportunities on a regular/daily basis.

CHAPTER 8

GIVING

FEEDBACK

KEY LEARNING POINTS

- Being able to give positive feedback
- Knowing how to avoid negative feedback
- Being able to deal with relationship difficulties
- Knowing how to encourage openness and honesty

GIVING POSITIVE FEEDBACK

Put the book down and think back to when you were last criticized. Picture the scene in your mind. See the face of the person criticizing you and hear the words again. Note how you are feeling and the thoughts that drift through your mind as you hear the criticism.

I doubt if you are enjoying remembering the experience. Though I cannot know how you feel when you are criticized I know that I usually feel angry, annoyed, belittled, and I try to deal with these feelings by seeing what I can learn from the experience, but I never enjoy criticism.

In giving positive feedback the aim is to be accurate in what we have to say and yet give the recipient of the feedback

I want to highlight this very important point about feelings interrupting people 'getting the message'.

a sense of comfort, so that they fully hear what we are saying without letting their feelings interrupt their listening.

There are skills in giving positive feedback. These include:

- being able to give praise;
- being able to encourage people;
- knowing how to avoid being patronizing;
- knowing how to dwell on the positive.

GIVING PRAISE

Praise is one of these gifts that we are unwilling to give and yearn to receive. Perhaps one of the reasons for this is that we are not attuned to looking for the good, to admire strength, but rather to searching out fault and weakness.

People ask you for criticism, but they only want praise.
Somerset Maugham

To give praise effectively you need to:

- recognize that something has been done that warrants praise;
- respond immediately;
- use simple words;
- be precise and neither understate or overstate your appreciation.

Here is an example:

I noted how well you handled that complaint and I want you to know that I appreciated your clarity and the way you were sympathetic and yet firm with the customer.

When praise is given in this straightforward way it confirms the actions people have taken and reinforces their learning and experience. If praise is overstated it has the opposite effect. Most of us are aware of how well we are performing and whether or not we deserve praise. So to receive it when we don't think we deserve it immediately changes it in our minds into sarcasm. Praise is a very important part of the process of

Here is another way of thinking about praise. If P stands for performance then see praise as 'P-raise'.

helping people to learn, and it has to be handled carefully and appropriately.

> **There is no such whetstone, to sharpen a good wit to learning as is praise.**
>
> **Roger Ascham**

ENCOURAGING PEOPLE

Encouragement has three elements:

- an expression of your belief that the other person can do it;
- support for the person through guidance and availability;
- patience and non-critical responses to 'miss-takes'.

BELIEF IN OTHERS

Your belief in other people's ability to do something, if repeated often enough and if supported by success in small steps, will lead to other people increasing their own self-belief.

Self-belief and self-esteem are important ingredients in creating people's confidence to do all the learning that success requires.

GUIDANCE AND AVAILABILITY

You cannot encourage someone if you are not there. On the other hand you can overdo it by being a constant presence leaning over someone's shoulder as he or she tries to perform. A happy balance has to be found by which you can offer guidance and be available if needed.

PATIENCE AND NON-CRITICAL RESPONSES

As I have said before, people will make 'miss-takes' when they are learning. Your patience will undoubtedly be tested over and over again as you help your people to perform and it can be hard to maintain a flow of non-critical feedback, yet this is exactly what you need to do to provide an encouraging atmosphere.

Stop for a moment and think about the last time you received the kind of encouragement described here. How did you feel and how did you respond?

Scenario – A step in the right direction

David and James work together. David is James's supervisor/coach. They have been negotiating a contract with a new customer who hasn't done business with the company before. James is having a problem.

James They are pressing for further cuts in our prices and insisting on quite a harsh penalty clause. I just don't seem to be able to budge them.

David I suggest you try to get them to focus on one thing at a time, but first of all try to make sure that these are the only two points outstanding.

James returns after more work with the prospective customer; he is no further forward.

David OK, so what would you like to do about it?

James Could you pay them a visit with me? I'm sure you could sort it out.

David What do you think I would do?

James You would be quite firm with them and just tell them straight what we are prepared to do.

David Right, well, I suggest you go and do that. I believe that you can do it and I am confident that if you don't worry about losing the deal you can succeed, and if you can't I will come with you next time.

This process of asking questions instead of giving answers is a major element of coaching (see Chapter 11).

James came back from his next meeting with an agreement within the acceptable range previously agreed with David. He was of course delighted, and David congratulated him on a job well done.

AVOIDING BEING PATRONIZING

There is a tendency when giving feedback, especially praise, to sound condescending and patronizing. This happens when we use language which tends to make us sound parental and judgemental. For example:

'I am very pleased with you for ...'
'I think you are working well.'
'I'm glad you've been able to grasp ...'
'I'm very satisfied with you.'

The problem is partly in the words we choose and partly in how we use and deliver them. The way to avoid being patronizing is to state what is happening and what we think about the work rather than the person. By concentrating on the work itself we avoid making any judgement about the person. Here is an example:

> I like the way that you spoke to Mrs Smith and listened to her reply. You could probably tell from her responses that you dealt with her complaint very well. It was a good piece of work.

By focusing on the work and the person's performance it is possible to be clear and direct without the risk of being patronizing or condescending.

DWELLING ON THE POSITIVE

One of the ways in which good positive feedback is spoilt is the tendency that some people have to sneak in a negative comment as an afterthought. Here is an example:

> I like the way that you spoke to Mrs Smith and listened to her reply. You could probably tell from her response that you dealt with her complaint very well. It was a good piece of work. It would be nice if you could do it more often.

Another way that people spoil a piece of good feedback is by using the word, but, to introduce a negative point. For example:

> The way you close sales is excellent and your success ratio is very high, but your after-sales support leaves a lot to be desired.

The opening positive comment is completely overtaken by

the final sneaky negative comment. It is important when giving feedback to separate the praiseworthy from the problematic so that each receives the appropriate focus and emphasis.

I want to emphasize this point about separating out feedback so that people can receive praise uncluttered by other feedback.

AVOIDING NEGATIVE FEEDBACK

Whether or not you choose to give negative feedback is entirely up to you. It can have the effect of motivating people to perform. To tell people that they can't do something may well motivate them to prove you are wrong. However, in my experience I have found that negative feedback tends to demotivate people; if they are told something often enough, people come to believe it.

I like to avoid negative feedback and I find it quite easy to do this by the simple approach of being simple, direct and non-critical. I can deal with almost any situation in a positive way by looking at what I want to happen rather than dwelling on what has happened, and to look at the activity and not the person.

Imagine what you would say to members of your staff who have avoided doing something you have asked them to do. You have reminded them several times and still the task has not been done. Think for a moment how you would feel. Then think about how you would tackle them.

Here is an approach I might take.

Be simple and state the obvious
'I have asked you several times to do ... and you have not done it yet; what's going on?'

Listen to the answer without commenting
'I'm sorry but I don't want to do it because it's something that one of the junior staff should do.'

Be direct and say what you feel
'I find your avoiding doing what I asked you to do quite frustrating and I wish that you had told me earlier about the

problem you are having. Now, what are we going to do about it?'

Agree a solution

'Well, I would have preferred you to ask someone junior to me to do it.'

'Well I didn't do that because everyone is so busy. OK, I tell you what – I'll do it and we'll just forget that I asked you.'

'No it's OK, I didn't realize we were so busy. I'll do it.'

'Are you sure?'

'Yes, I'm sure.'

'OK, good, thanks.'

This example could have gone a number of ways but whichever way it might have gone the manager could still have kept the feedback positive. The alternative might have been to get into some kind of power or status argument which undoubtedly would have become negative.

There are two other aspects of keeping feedback positive which I think are important. These are:

- deliberately using criticism as a weapon;
- projecting our own feelings onto others.

DELIBERATELY USING CRITICISM

We can and, much to our discredit, do use criticism to hurt and wound others. Our need to do this is in some measure determined by how we ourselves have been subjected to criticism in our past. That we do it at all is much to be regretted and it can always be avoided, no matter how significant the provocation.

Using criticism in this way is our last defence and a rather mean one at that. It is because we can see no way to deal with the matter in a more positive way, or because we choose not to. Criticism is in effect a failure to find a more appropriate way of dealing with the issue. I believe that when we criticize in a negative way we diminish the person we criticize and we diminish ourselves for having to resort to criticism. What people call constructive criticism is in fact positive feedback.

Sometimes people want to be critical and hurtful, possibly out of frustration, and they call what they do 'constructive' to hide their real intent.

PROJECTING OUR OWN FEELINGS ONTO OTHERS

If I say to someone 'You frustrate me,' I am in fact saying, 'I am frustrated' but rather than own up and be responsible for how I am feeling, I blame the other person. This is a common occurrence, especially in an organizational setting. There are many situations in which people are criticized and blamed for the feelings their managers are having.

Scenario – Bringing feelings to work

Rosemary, a department head, has arrived at work after having had a row the previous evening with her husband about her working late and the house being a mess. She has had a sleepless night and is feeling unfairly treated, angry, upset and scared about what the outcome might be. She looks in her in-tray and sees a memo from her boss about a complaint he has received about her department. She gathers her staff in the conference room.

'Shut the door,' she snaps at the last person in. Waving the memo, she says, 'This arrived from my boss this morning and I am upset and angry to think that I have to put up with complaints like this because of your sloppy attitudes to your work. It's not fair that I have to carry the can for you lot and it's going to stop.'

Her staff are surprised. No one has any idea what she is talking about. What she has said to them is a projection of how she is feeling and the criticism and blame that she received from her husband. She even uses virtually the same words that her husband used to her: 'sloppy attitude to the housework'. She pours her anger and frustration onto her staff which is extremely unfair and inappropriate.

In this scenario Rosemary has at least two other options. She could be aware of how she is feeling and deal with the memo later when her feelings don't get in the way. Or she could tell

It is easy to refer to people who are having difficulties as 'difficult people'. This causes blame and the focus of attention to be attached to the person instead of the difficulty.

her staff how she is feeling and why and then ask someone to deal with the memo by finding out what it's about. Either way she is owning her feelings and being responsible for them.

Even when your feelings have been influenced by things that happen at work it is still important to own them and to share how you are feeling with your staff. This is a key to dealing with difficulties.

DEALING WITH RELATIONSHIP DIFFICULTIES

When a difficulty arises it usually generates feelings between the people involved. These can get in the way of finding a solution, especially if each of the people concerned is projecting feelings onto the other person.

There is a quite straightforward way of dealing with this situation. It is the four-step approach and goes like this:

1. State what happens – 'When you do ...'
2. State how you feel – 'I feel ...'
3. State why – 'because ...'
4. State what you want – 'I would prefer it if you ...'

Here is an example of two people dealing with a difficulty using the four-step approach:

'When you don't arrive on time I feel angry because I have to fill in for you and I would prefer it if you were here on time or let me know you are going to be late.'

'When you shout at me because I am late I feel upset because you don't know about my problems getting Jimmy to school and I would prefer it if we could agree for me to start half an hour later.'

This form of communication is very powerful because it is open and honest; feelings are owned instead of projected and each person's point of view is heard by the other. It is a simple formula for dealing with most relationship difficulties in the workplace and you will notice that it is totally positive feedback.

OPENNESS AND HONESTY

One of the problems in giving good positive feedback is not to leave anything unsaid. This is much more difficult to do than to say. Imagine the problems that might arise if you were to speak your thoughts without censoring them. However, this is not what I mean. What I do mean is saying what you want to say. Here is a short conversation where neither person is saying what they want to say.

Mary   Oh heavens, it's raining and I have to walk home tonight.

Joan   I can give you a lift if you want.

Mary   No it's all right really, the walk will do me good.

Joan   Are you sure?

Mary   Yes honestly.

The outcome is that Mary walks home and gets sopping wet and is annoyed that Joan didn't give her a lift. Joan feels guilty for not taking Mary but blames her for insisting that she didn't need a lift. Here is the revised version.

Mary   Oh heavens, it's raining. Could you give me a lift?

Joan   Well it's a bit out of my way, but OK, seeing as it's raining.

Mary   Thanks, I appreciate it. Perhaps I can return the favour sometime.

Joan   OK, I'll hold you to that.

One of the problems that people have in being open and direct is that it leaves them exposed. It offers few escape paths down the, 'I didn't really mean that' or the 'Why didn't you say' variety. People have to 'come clean' and this can make them feel vulnerable to less open people.

Giving feedback is all about saying it as it is, focusing on the positive and leaving people feeling better informed and feeling better.

ACTION LIST – GIVING FEEDBACK

1. Talk to your staff as a group and ask them how they react to criticism. Encourage an open and honest debate.
2. At the same meeting ask your staff what they:
   (a) like about the way you give feedback,
   (b) dislike about the way you give feedback.
3. Find a way to practise the four-step approach with one of your staff.
4. Ask the members of your staff how you could encourage them in their work.
5. Stop whatever you are doing and focus on what you are feeling. Be aware of how you are sitting, sense the feel of your clothes on your skin. Focus your attention on yourself and notice the feedback process.

PART 3

FACILITATION AND COACHING

The idea that managers are more effective when they empower other people rather than direct them is growing as more and more managers experience it for themselves. In this book and the series we are endeavouring to provide information in a way that will help you to facilitate learning and coach people in implementing what they learn. For us to be successful in this aim it is important that we spend some time looking at facilitation and coaching.

Part 3 offers four chapters that focus on the topics of facilitation, empowering others, the coaching cycle and performance support.

You may find that this material invites you to operate in ways that are different from those you have experienced so far in your career as a manager. I suggest that you neither reject them out of hand, nor jump on the bandwagon, but that you consider the information carefully in conjunction with discussions with your people. Then, if you think there is merit in the ideas, try them out and experiment with ways in which you can be different. Assess what you think from your experience.

CHAPTER 9

THE SCOPE OF FACILITATION

KEY LEARNING POINTS

- ■ Knowing what facilitation is
- ■ Understanding the facilitation spectrum
- ■ Knowing that facilitation is about helping and supporting people
- ■ Being able to let people 'get on with it'

KNOWING WHAT FACILITATION IS

Modern people management is much more a process of facilitation than direction. People respond better to the empowerment of facilitation than the disempowerment of instruction. Supervision is now a process of getting people to share a 'super-vision' rather than telling them what to do. This changing environment presents managers with the challenge of changing their style of management.

There is nothing magical about facilitation, yet when people come into contact with good facilitation there is a sense of something magical happening. This is usually because the people involved are discovering things about themselves that had previously been dormant.

See John Heider's book *The Tao of Leadership* (Heider, 1987) to discover some of the magic.

Good facilitation is the process of guiding people towards their own wisdom rather than trying to instil someone else's 'wisdom' in them. It is a process of learning and growth.

There are many similarities between what people often describe as leadership, and facilitation. These similarities are to do with the way that the process is carried through. However, for some people leadership means being able to direct and move others along a path that the leader decides is appropriate. This is only one form of leadership. It is sometimes useful but is often not very effective.

Facilitation is about empowering people to take control and responsibility for their own efforts and achievements. If we grow and develop as people we do so because we make a choice to do so. We cannot be 'developed' by others.

Good leaders know this. Around 500 BC Lao Tzu is believed to have written the Tao Teh Ching. It describes a philosophy for life, 'The Way'; here is Chapter 17 about leadership:

> **A leader is best**
> **When people barely know that he exists,**
> **Not so good when people obey and acclaim him,**
> **Worst when they despise him.**
> **'Fail to honour people,**
> **They fail to honour you;'**
> **But of a good leader, who talks little,**
> **When his work is done, his aim fulfilled,**
> **They will all say, 'We did this ourselves.'**

Facilitation echoes this message from Lao Tzu by trying to determine 'the way' that people want to go, and by trying to encourage and support them in this process. This does mean sometimes leading from the front, but it is how we do this rather than what we are doing that is important. Sometimes we have to lead from within the work group, by example and participation rather than persuasion. And there are times when it is important to lead from the back, to follow, and by following willingly and with skill to enable people to lead.

The three leadership positions are out in front; from within; and from the back.

In his book *The Tao of Leadership*, John Heider, building on the writing of Lao Tzu, says:

What we call leadership consists mainly of knowing how to follow. The wise leader stays in the background and facilitates other people's process.

(Heider, 1987)

What I have said so far about facilitation may seem at odds with the dynamic action–oriented approach often suggested in management training programmes. Consider to what extent my description of facilitation differs from how you manage and help your people to perform.

The word 'facilitate' comes from the Latin *facilis* which means 'to make easy'. The dictionary definitions vary. Here are three:

1. To free from difficulties and obstacles, to make easy.
2. To lessen the labour of.
3. To render easier, to promote, help forward.

Here is my definition of facilitation:

Facilitation is the provision of opportunities, resources, encouragement and support for your people to succeed in achieving their objectives, and to do this through enabling them to take control and responsibility for the way they proceed.

THE FACILITATION SPECTRUM

Facilitation consists of a range of ways of interacting with people that can be called upon as the situation demands. Figure 9.1 depicts this range of options from 'doing nothing' to 'directing'. This facilitation spectrum is intended as a guide to possibilities.

There is no good, bad, worst or better in these options. However, as we move down the spectrum our input into and control of the activity of people increases and we face the danger of disempowering them. The success of any

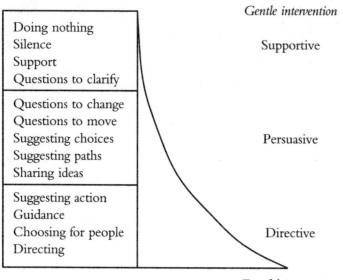

Gentle intervention

Doing nothing Silence Support Questions to clarify	Supportive
Questions to change Questions to move Suggesting choices Suggesting paths Sharing ideas	Persuasive
Suggesting action Guidance Choosing for people Directing	Directive

Forceful intervention

FIGURE 9.1: The facilitation spectrum

intervention technique is judged by its outcome and not by how 'clever' the intervention is.

Facilitation is mainly concerned with serving people rather than being served by them and in particular getting them to do things for themselves. This approach to facilitation can be quite frustrating for some people.

It is hard for some managers to perceive themselves to be the 'servants' of their staff. They want it to be the other way round.

Scenario – The workshop

It was mid-afternoon on Wednesday and we were all sitting round the pool having tea. The day so far had been very relaxed and everybody seemed to be enjoying themselves. There had been a lot of social conversation and a good deal of talk about the workshop. Derek was talking to Sid and Michael, but most of the group could hear.

'What really frustrates me is the way Trevor won't directly answer questions. I've stopped asking him because

I know he'll only ask me what I think, but I'm still frustrated by it. And not having a programme frustrates me to hell.'

Sid and Michael were laughing and the whole conversation was light-hearted. They both agreed that they found this form of facilitation frustrating, but for different reasons. Other members of the group started to say what they found frustrating and our pleasant tea round the pool became a discussion about frustration. So I went for a swim.

When I came to the side after a couple of lengths I could hear Derek still talking about frustration. He walked over to the pool and spoke to me.

'You just did it again, didn't you?'

'Did what?' I asked him.

'You frustrated me on purpose, didn't you?'

'How on earth did I do that?' I asked him.

'Well, we were having a discussion about facilitation and frustration and you just went for a swim.'

'You didn't want me to do that, then?' I asked.

'No, I wanted you to comment about what we were saying to join in the discussion,' he said.

'But I didn't want to do that, I wanted a swim, and anyway, how was I supposed to know what you wanted when you didn't tell me?' I said.

He shook his head and walked away, clearly puzzled and still somewhat frustrated.

> Derek is really frustrated by his own lack of clarity in being able to get what he wants.

HELPING AND SUPPORTING PEOPLE

There are three things that most people find very difficult to say, especially in a working environment. These are:

- I am wrong
- I don't know
- I need help

Facilitation means encouraging people to say these things so that they can take responsibility for their own growth and development. Because these three things are rarely said, the manager working as a facilitator has to be able to pick them up by paying close attention to what is going on. The skills needed for doing this are:

Listening in an open and quiet way. This enables you to hear what is happening and to be aware of the feelings and emotions that lie behind what others are saying. It also gives you a basis for the choices that you can make about what is happening, how it is happening, and what you might want to do.

Questioning in an enquiring and learning way. When you do this, and when you listen quietly and attentively to the replies, you are able to learn and to understand what is happening. You can then make choices about what you do.

Communicating your thoughts, feelings and ideas clearly about what is happening. You are unable to do this unless you listen and understand what is happening. When you do this you can contribute and share whatever you believe might be of help. It also gives you a sense of freedom to act as you think fit.

Acting in your chosen way and in the best interests of those you are with so as to achieve shared objectives. When you act, you choose and take responsibility for what you do. This choice is based on your clear understanding of what is happening and on the clarity with which you express your thoughts, feelings and emotions about what is happening.

Reviewing what is happening is concerned with listening, questioning and communicating with others about **what is happening NOW**. By constantly checking what is happening in the here and now, you can stay grounded in the present rather than keep replaying the past or fantasizing about the future.

Adapting to the changing conditions in which you are living and working. When you are aware of how things are changing you can choose to adapt your actions accordingly. This allows you the freedom to change your mind to adjust what you do to suit the particular needs of the moment rather than stick to previously relevant but no longer appropriate ideas.

Bring your people together for a discussion about how you can help them perform. If you have done the other exercises suggested so far they will be ready for a lively discussion. During this discussion use the six activities described above to facilitate the meeting. Try to intervene as little as possible.

LETTING OTHERS GET ON WITH IT

The facilitator's presence, or lack of presence, has a direct impact on the group. Yet 'being there' can be exercised in a variety of ways. From the 'invisible facilitator' to the 'charismatic leader', there are many different ways of 'being there'. Good facilitators will be able to move along the facilitation spectrum as is most appropriate to enable their people to keep moving towards their objectives.

The first key to 'being there' is to be *fully myself* in every way possible. I need to be able to respond openly and in a real way so that the group can see there is no pretence. Whatever I am feeling about what is happening is shared with the group; they become conscious of my presence, not because of my repeated and overpowering interaction, but because of their awareness of my sustained conscious attention.

Sustained conscious attention is presence

> **The best work often seems idiotically simple to group members who are unaccustomed to this sort of leadership. Yet a great deal happens. Perhaps it looks as if the leader is only sitting there and has no idea what to do. But it is just this lack of needless intervention that permits the group to grow and be fertile.**
>
> **(Heider, 1987)**

The group experience my presence as being a support for them, without being a crutch for their vulnerability. They recognize that they have my respect and trust to go in whichever direction they choose, and they know that I am there purely to assist them to do just that. They recognize that

I am there to sponsor their objectives and that this is the only thing I want them to achieve. Because of this they know that when I am still and quiet they are being guided by their own inner direction-finders.

It is in this way that people take responsibility and find their power.

Scenario – The workshop 2

We assembled after lunch. Each person was to run a session and I checked that everyone had had enough time to prepare. Jennifer said she thought that she would never be ready, however much time she had. There was a general thought that perhaps more time for preparation would be useful.

'OK, I have an idea,' I said, and then I stayed silent.

'Well, what is it then?' Derek asked after a couple of minutes.

'Why don't you decide how much time you want, and how we are going to use the rest of the time remaining for the workshop? In that way you will be able to work out how much time you need for what.'

They agreed that this seemed a good idea and then they sat quietly waiting, I imagined for me to say or do something.

'OK, well, while you sort out what you are going to do I'm going to get a cup of tea,' I said, standing and walking to the door. 'I'll be back shortly,' I called over my shoulder.

I went and put the kettle on and wandered into the kitchen to talk to the chef about the dinner that evening. As it was the last dinner of the workshop, I was organizing a rather special menu with wine and so on. About half an hour later I returned to the group. I entered the room and walked silently to a chair and sat down.

The group were in the middle of an animated discussion. Sid was standing by a flip chart with a programme for the rest of Thursday and Friday on it.

Michael was arguing that there needed to be at least an hour for closing the workshop. I noticed that the programme was pretty tight, and went on until 5.00 pm on Friday evening. I sat quietly and listened to the debate.

'I think we have spent long enough talking about the programme,' Jennifer said. 'Why don't we get on with it and see where we are up to later this evening, instead of trying to work every minute out in advance.'

'Well, I think we need to plan carefully because of the limited time,' Michael responded.

'Excuse me,' Greg said, 'but perhaps we could aim to start the rest of the programme after the tea break, in 10 minutes.'

'OK, then,' Sid said, 'let's just complete this plan and then stop.'

'Right,' Michael said, 'so if we allow an hour for closing, and an hour before that for assessment it means we need to stop the sessions at teatime tomorrow.'

'I'll go with that,' Derek said.

'So will I,' Doreen added.

'OK, that seems to do it,' Sid said, and he sat down.

'So let's have tea,' Joe said, and we all went for tea.

Choosing the point on the spectrum from which to operate is a key skill of facilitation.

In the above scenario I acted as an 'invisible facilitator'. I wasn't even there in a physical sense but I was there in a spiritual sense, having left the group to complete a task which I trusted they would do. The group recognized my respect and trust in leaving them to get on with it. An alternative approach would have been to lead from the front and to have guided the group towards a programme that I felt was both desirable and achievable. I could easily have done this but I imagine that there would have been a different level of commitment to my guided programme than there was for the group's own programme.

My role in being there is to be completely aware of what is happening so that I can respond in the most appropriate way. The group have to have the confidence that through my 'being there' they will be able to explore and develop in whatever way they want.

ACTION LIST – THE SCOPE OF FACILITATION

1. Using the facilitation spectrum, indicate where on the spectrum you normally operate with your staff. It may be a range rather than a single point.
2. Now ask your staff to indicate on the spectrum where they mostly experience your style of intervention.
3. Talk to your staff about the three things people don't say:
   (a) I am wrong
   (a) I don't know
   (c) I need help
   and discuss the implications of saying them.
4. How much do you manage by 'being there'? Ask your people if they experience you as 'being there' even when you are not present.

CHAPTER 10

EMPOWERING OTHERS

KEY LEARNING POINTS

- Knowing about levels of power
- Being able to get people to own their power
- Being able to avoid giving people your power
- Being able to not take other people's power

DIFFERENT LEVELS OF POWER

Most people are able to exercise two levels of power – personal power and role power – and for some there is a third level, reflected power.

Personal power is associated with confidence and self-esteem and enables people to make choices and decisions about their own lives in a way that ensures they live as they would wish. People with a strong sense of personal power are able to listen to the ideas and suggestions of other people, to weigh up the advice they receive, and then act to suit themselves without being unduly swayed in the direction others might want them to be.

Role power is the power people have because of the role they happen to have at the time. It is possible to have several roles, each of which carries a certain power. For example, you could be a father or mother, a manager, a husband or wife, captain of the hockey team, and so on. In each of these roles there is a certain designated, or assumed, power. This might be specified by the organization for whom we play the role, or implied from our experience or the expectation of others.

Reflected power is a level of power exercised by those close to 'powerful' people. They bask in the power that emanates from their more powerful companions. Personal assistants often operate with the reflected role power of their bosses. Children can express the reflected power of their parents – being the son of a prime minister, for example, can carry with it a lot of reflected power. Husbands and wives often operate with the reflected power of their partners.

This reflected power is often mistaken as the personal or role power of the individuals themselves rather than of the person they are close to. The problem with this is the loss of awareness as to whose power is being exercised. Recognizing and using reflected power is a valuable attribute and it needs full awareness of what they are doing on the part of the people using the reflected power.

> Ambassadors carry the role power of their position, they have their own personal power, and the reflected power of the country they represent.

In exercising power we all operate with a combination of personal power and role power and sometimes reflected power. The extent to which we are able to fully utilize our power depends on many factors including our upbringing, education, training, experience, the role we have, the people around us, and so on.

Pause for a moment and think about all the roles you play in your life. What is the extent of your role power?

Now think for a moment about your personal power. How would you rate yourself on a scale from 'very powerful' to 'not powerful'?

Now check if you might be exercising someone else's reflected power.

So, if we all have access to these levels of power what do we mean when we talk about 'empowering' people? Write in the space opposite your definition of 'empowerment'.

Empowerment is the_____

_____

_____

_____

_____

GETTING PEOPLE TO OWN THEIR POWER

If people have 'personal power' and 'role power' how do they disempower themselves? Here are a few clues:

- When we exercise power we have to take responsibility for what we do.
- When we make choices we have to live with the consequences.
- When I use my power other people criticize and blame me for what happens.
- Exercising power can be scary.

Many people find life more comfortable and have an artificial sense of security if other people exercise power on their behalf. They do in fact give away their power and unfortunately, there are plenty of people willing to take it from them. I say 'unfortunately' because in effect those who take the power only receive it by dint of their role. This forsaken power can in no way enhance the recipients' personal power which is evidenced when they leave the role.

This 'loss' of power is evident when senior executives retire or senior managers are made redundant. With the loss of role they lose their power.

Scenario – The meeting

The meeting had been running for about an hour when an issue arose which personally involved the Chair. It was suggested that the Chair should vacate the Chair for the discussion of this issue. This happened. What was particularly noticeable was the way that the Chair, now acting as a member of the committee, seemed to exercise only a fraction of the power she normally exercised as Chair, and the rest of the committee seemed to be exercising much more individual power than they did when the Chair was running the meeting.

There are three steps you can use with your people to get them to own their power.

1. Discuss the issue of power and look at the extent of power and the way it is exercised by your people. Separate personal power from role power.
2. Look at your own power issues and see what aspects of your power could be exercised by your people, not as reflected power, but as their own role power. If the power is not rightly yours give it back to the person to whom it belongs.
3. Encourage your people to own their power and refuse to take their power when they offer it to you.

Here are some of the ways that people give their power away:

- What would you do?
- I just can't do it; would you do it please?
- It's really up to you.
- You're the Chair.
- I don't have a choice.
- If that's what you think I'd better do it.
- What do you want me to do about ...?

In each case you can refuse to take their power by getting

them to act for themselves. See if you can think of ways of dealing with each of the examples above.

NOT GIVING PEOPLE YOUR POWER

As others may give away their power, so might you. Even with an awareness of the possibility of giving away our power we can still do so.

The important thing to be clear about is: *whose power are you exercising?*

It is very helpful to be able to clearly separate out your personal power, your role power and any reflected power that you might be exercising. This will help to answer the question about whose power it is. If you are ever in doubt you can stop and consider what is happening and decide who should be exercising power over events.

Of course there will be moments when people are competing for power, but remember they can only compete for role power. Your personal power is yours unless you give it away. I have always been interested in the question – do leaders lead because followers follow, or vice versa?

NOT TAKING OTHER PEOPLE'S POWER

There is a great temptation to take someone else's power when it is offered to us. There is an immediate feeling of superiority and one's ego gets a significant boost. It is possible to fall into this trap even if you don't want to take the power. The trainer who stands in front of an audience is often the recipient of the power of the audience. Some trainers enjoy this sense of power and talk about the 'buzz' they get from training. The frustration of teenagers at school has a lot to do with their newly discovered personal power being taken from them temporarily by teachers.

Some managers take the power of their staff and bask in their feelings of self-importance. Politicians deliberately take the power of the people through public oratory. They then exercise the power of the people on behalf of the people. Far

> **Many difficulties arise because of the lack of clarity attached to power issues.**

too many politicians forget whose power it is and act as if it is their own.

You can avoid taking other people's power away from them by acting in three ways:

1. Recognize when people are deliberately or unintentionally declining to use their own power.
2. Be aware of the extent of your own personal and role power and any reflected power that you might use.
3. Refuse to exercise anyone else's power.

You will be aware of Lord Acton's famous saying, 'Power tends to corrupt and absolute power corrupts absolutely'.

Scenario – Maintaining power boundaries

George was talking to his boss Sheila about interviewing several candidates for the vacant post of assistant manager.

George It would help me a great deal if you could interview the candidates with me.

Sheila How would it help you?

George Well, I don't want to hire someone you will not be happy with.

Sheila Who is the new recruit going to report to and work closely with?

George (sounding puzzled) Well, me, of course.

Sheila So don't you think you are the right person to make the selection?

George (not sounding convinced) Yes, I suppose so.

Sheila Look George, this appointment is your responsibility and you have the power to hire who you want. I am not going to take your power by sharing the decision with you, or making it for you. I will support you, but it is your decision.

George OK, that's pretty clear.

The question of maintaining power boundaries is fundamental to empowerment. If we see empowerment as the process by which people take power, then it has three components:

- realization and acceptance of personal power;
- investment of power in the role being carried out;
- the extent to which access is available to reflected power.

It is these three components which determine the power boundaries.

ACTION LIST – EMPOWERING OTHERS

1. Bring your people together and talk to them about the three levels of power. Ask them to look in turn at their personal power, their role power and any reflected power they may use.
2. Look at your own power on these three levels and see how it fits with your staff's power.
3. Ask your people how you take their power.
4. Discuss how you think they give you their power.
5. Working with your people establish the power boundaries that exist, that is, yours and each of theirs.

CHAPTER 11

THE COACHING CYCLE

KEY LEARNING POINTS

- Knowing that coaching is about empowerment
- Understanding the stages of coaching
- Recognizing that coaching is about asking questions not giving advice
- Knowing that coaching is a step-by-step process
- Understanding that coaching is a partnership

COACHING IS ABOUT EMPOWERMENT

Perhaps the most important aspect of coaching is getting people to believe in themselves. The idea that *what they are trying to achieve is possible* is central to effective coaching. Coaching also includes encouragement for individuals to apply with existing knowledge and skills more effectively and thus improve their performance.

There is a distinct difference between training and coaching, although the two quite often get confused. The following definitions of each are given purely to indicate the basis of the difference between them.

Training

The provision of opportunities for people to *gain new knowledge and skills*.

Coaching

The provision of support and guidance for people to *use their existing knowledge and skills more effectively*.

In coaching there is no intention to 'train', but during coaching you may find that the understanding and/or insight of your people improves and that they discover more about the subtleties of applying their knowledge and skills to their work.

There can be a 'training' element in coaching when coaches make suggestions and/or give technical pointers. However, the aim of coaching is development, not skill acquisition.

THE STAGES OF COACHING

Coaching is a cycle of activities which may focus on the whole job or just a part of the job of the person you are coaching.

The coaching cycle consists of five stages and is depicted in Figure 11.1 in the form of a wave which rises and falls as the energy ebbs and flows.

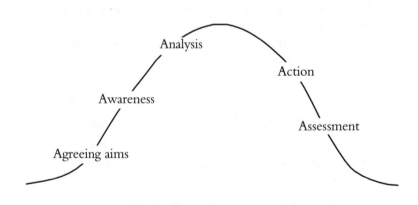

Analysis

Action

Awareness

Assessment

Agreeing aims

FIGURE 11.1: The coaching cycle

AGREEING AIMS

The first stage of the coaching process is to agree the aims of the coaching activity. This need not be a lengthy process. The focus should be on that part of the job-holder's performance that has been selected for attention. The primary aim will be to improve performance. For coaching to be successful it is necessary to agree more detailed specific aims for the various elements that make up the area identified for improvement. It is also important for these aims to be measurable and have agreed completion dates.

AWARENESS

It is important that you as coach and the person you are coaching are aware of what is happening. As coach it is helpful if you are able to guide job-holders to a clearer understanding of what they are doing. Don't make assumptions. Talk with the people being coached about what you see happening and try to get them to understand and agree.

Clarity about *what* is happening at the moment is perhaps the most important aspect of coaching. It is not necessary to know *why* it is happening. What is important is to know how we can do things differently to improve. Knowing what is happening now is the starting point in recognizing the gap between where we are and where we want to be.

See the questioning approach (Figure 11.2) later in this chapter.

ANALYSIS

Analysing what you have observed and what the job-holder has experienced is the next critical step. It is from this analysis that you and the job-holder can discuss the options and evaluate them to determine what can be done differently to improve.

If the analysis is an effective two-way interaction between you and the job-holder, then there is every chance that job-holders will recognize things they can do for themselves.

Remember, during the analysis stage it is essential to make sure that both coach and job-holder learn from the experience. It is not about finding fault or focusing on errors.

See Chapter 8 on giving non-critical feedback.

ACTION

In coaching the action stage is clearly seen as an opportunity to learn rather than a test of ability. To make the action effective it is important that job-holders know clearly what is expected of them and have the support and experience of you as coach. The encouragement to try new things is essential for improving performance. *Taking action is the essence of performance.*

ASSESSMENT

The final stage of the coaching process is the assessment of the performance in a form that will help the job-holder to improve. This is where positive encouragement is so important. Being honest and giving non-critical feedback is essential.

Whatever system of assessment is agreed and understood it should be used as a review mechanism to evaluate the degree of success achieved, the learning experienced and further opportunities for improvement. The assessment stage is followed by a resting stage which enables both the coach and the person being coached to reflect on their learning and development.

From my experience I recommend doing the assessment in three stages:

- an overall evaluation of how well the performer did;
- some indication of the good elements of the performance;
- suggestions for improvement.

In the coaching process it is important we recognize that people being coached may often have greater skill and ability than the coach, but without the critical eye and the knowing experience of the coach they may find it difficult to improve. For example, Wimbledon finalists are usually far better players than their coaches, but the coaching can make all the difference. The whole coaching approach is for someone who is trusted and who has **knowledge** and **experience**, to help someone less experienced but with skill and talent to develop.

ASKING QUESTIONS

Successful coaching is achieved by a process of asking questions rather than giving technical advice, though this may be done as well. The purpose of the questions varies but in general they are aimed at generating awareness of what is going on and clarity of understanding, as well as inviting the people being coached to take responsibility for their performance.

Figure 11.2 is a schedule of questions for the five steps.

PROCESS STAGES	QUESTIONS ASKED leads to	INFORMATION GAINED
Agreeing aims	■ What are we trying to achieve? ■ When are we going to do it? ■ How will we know we have succeeded?	Clear objectives Agreed dates Measurement
Awareness	■ What is happening now? ■ What are the consequences? ■ What do we want to be different?	Clear picture of current actions Effect of current actions Gap between where we are and where we want to be
Analysis	■ What can we change? ■ What are the options? ■ How can we change it? ■ What are the risks? ■ What are the barriers?	Identify possibilities Broaden vision Seek solutions Evaluate choices Obstacles to overcome
Action	■ What are we going to do? ■ Who is going to do what? ■ When are we going to do it? ■ What do we need to help us?	Clear action steps Agree responsibilities Agree milestones Determine support
NOW DO IT		
Assessment	■ What actually happened? ■ Was this what we wanted? ■ What have we learned? ■ How can we improve?	Clarify outcomes Evaluate degree of success Discoveries made Establish further potential

FIGURE 11.2: The coaching process

Scenario – The Service and Sales meeting

Michael is running a Service and Sales meeting for the first time after having attended a course on running meetings. He is aware that it is part of a coaching exercise. The scenario starts before the meeting and continues afterwards. Margaret is Michael's manager. They are having a discussion about the meeting and the way Margaret will support Michael.

Margaret The important thing about the meeting is that it is a basis for you to develop your skills. I will be here to offer support and encouragement and afterwards we can discuss how it went, share our views and agree how to take it further.

Michael I'm feeling very nervous about the meeting, and about getting stuck, or having problems.

Margaret Well that's quite understandable, I was nervous at my first Service and Sales meeting, but I found that by preparing thoroughly and using what I had learned at my course I didn't get stuck. I don't think you will either, if you prepare well and use what you've learned. And remember I'll be available.

Michael Thanks. It helps me to know that.

Margaret OK. So remember what we are doing – at this stage we are not focusing on any particular aspect of running meetings. We want to see how you do in all areas. I expect that you will handle some aspects well and others perhaps not so well, but of course we don't know what these are at the moment.

Michael Thanks. I think I'm ready now.

Two days later the staff are gathered for the weekly Service and Sales meeting.

Margaret Good afternoon everyone, while I am attending

the meeting this week Michael is going to lead it. OK Michael, over to you.

Michael Thanks Margaret, well I suggest we start by ... oh, before we do, can I check that everyone has seen the sales figures?

There is a general agreement and so Michael continues.

Michael Well, perhaps I can ask you to comment, Geoff, about the figures for personal loans.

Geoff I think it's quite clear that our customers are not getting the message about our competitive rates at the moment. I think we need to change our advertising.

Michael Well that may be so, but does that explain why we are so far behind target?

Geoff (in a somewhat aggressive tone) No, not completely, the referrals we are getting haven't really established the customer's needs, so we waste a lot of time sorting out what they really want. Anyway, why pick on me, other areas are way down as well.

Michael I wasn't picking on you, it just seemed that you were making excuses rather than saying what the difficulties are. You have given two reasons, neither of which have anything to do with you. What I would like to hear at the next meeting is what you can do about it, not what you can't. Now Peter, how about the mortgage side of things?

Peter Well, we have had several difficulties. First we have had staff problems because of flu, and second we don't have sufficient information on the new mortgage package – and don't tell me these are excuses, because these are the facts.

Michael OK, OK, calm down. I just want us to focus on what we can do.

Peter Well, your attitude isn't helping.

Michael I'm sorry if that's how you feel, but I am keen

> to make sure we agree some action rather than listen to a lot of excuses for poor performance.
>
> **Peter** It's all right for you to play high and mighty. Credit cards are easy to sell.
>
> **Michael** That's not fair ...
>
> **Margaret** Michael, we don't seem to be progressing in this area. Perhaps we can move on.
>
> The meeting continued until everyone had reported and each individual had agreed action for the following week. Michael then closed the meeting. Afterwards he met Margaret in her office.
>
> **Margaret** Well, how do you think it went?
>
> **Michael** Not so good, I got really tense and Peter didn't help.
>
> **Margaret** OK. On the plus side you got clear action plans sorted out for everybody, and you didn't just accept their excuses. However, there were some obvious difficulties. Now what I want you to do is to go over the meeting in your mind and to think about what you could have done differently, especially in the way you interacted with your colleagues. Let's meet on Wednesday to talk about it. Is that OK?
>
> **Michael** Yes, OK. Thanks, Margaret.

In the scenario above Michael has made a good start. At their Wednesday meeting Margaret and Michael agreed that there are at least six different areas in which Michael could improve. To address all six issues at this stage would be offputting for Michael and instead of feeling encouraged he may feel discouraged. Michael and his coach Margaret have decided that the first important step for him to take is to improve the way that he handles the interaction between people at the meeting. Margaret agrees that Michael needs to start here because it will affect everything else he tries to improve.

Scenario – The Service and Sales meeting (Part 2)

This is Michael's second Service and Sales meeting. Margaret and Michael have agreed that, of the six areas needing attention, he should focus on his interactions with others. The six areas are:

- opening the meeting and defining aims;
- focusing on key issues and keeping to the point;
- dealing with confrontation;
- making interventions;
- **interactions with others**;
- summarizing the meeting.

Michael Hello everyone, Margaret has asked me to lead the meeting again. What do you think we should focus on today?

Betty I would like us to consider more sales training.

Michael OK, anything else?

Peter Yes. I'd like a policy decision on the use of the tax notes that were circulated this week. Are we going to give them to customers or not?

Michael I don't think we can make a decision like that here ...

Peter Well, somebody needs to.

Michael (glaring at Peter) Any more points to consider?

There are no further suggestions and so Michael continues.

Michael Perhaps we could go round the table and ask each of you to report on sales for the week.

Betty OK I'll start ...

Each person reports to the meeting. Michael listens, takes notes and asks one or two questions to clarify points. When everyone has spoken he asks for general comments about sales performance.

Geoff Well, I don't think we've done too badly considering the current climate.

Michael What do you mean, Geoff?

Geoff People are not too excited about investing or borrowing; the whole economy is sluggish.

Michael That may be, but what are we going to do about increasing sales to our customers? I'm sure there must be scope.

Peter If we could get our act together we might stand some chance.

Michael (with a sharp edge to his voice) And exactly what is that supposed to mean?

Peter I think we need more explanatory leaflets and ...

Michael So you don't have to talk to customers, just send them away with something to read ...

Peter You know I don't mean that.

Michael Well, what *do* you mean?

Peter These tax notes for example, it's easier to explain when you have something to refer to.

Michael All right, so what do you suggest for the tax notes?

Peter Well, I think we should refer to them, and if customers ask for a copy we should give them one.

Mary Yes, I agree that's a good point.

Betty I agree too. It makes sense to do that.

Michael OK. Let's address that issue.

The meeting continues until suggestions for action have been agreed and Michael closes the meeting. He then meets Margaret.

Margaret Well, how do you think it went this time?

Michael Better I think, but Peter is still driving me mad.

Margaret Yes, you did seem to have some difficulty with him, but on the whole I thought your interaction was better this week, and you involved everyone more than at your first meeting.

Michael But what can I do about Peter?

> **Margaret** What would you like to do?
> **Michael** I'd like things to be better between us.
> **Margaret** Yes, you're right, if we ignore the problem it will only get worse, so how do you think you can improve your contact with Peter?
>
> Margaret then helped Michael to explore the nature of the difficulty and options for making changes.

Exercise – Coaching is a process

In each of the two scenarios two different things are happening at the same time. One is the Service and Sales meeting, the other is coaching. It is important that the coach should concentrate on the coaching *process* and the person being coached. Michael should focus on the *content* of the Service and Sales meeting and learning about his interactions with others.

1. Go through each of the scenarios again. Imagine that you are Michael's coach. Mark in the text of the scenario the points at which you believe each of the five coaching stages come into play.
2. Using the five stages of the coaching process outline where you would go from here to help Michael resolve the difficulties with Peter.

Agreeing aims

_____

_____

_____

Awareness

_____

_____

_____

Analysis

_____

_____

_____

Action

_____

_____

_____

Assessment

_____

_____

_____

Use this exercise as the basis for a discussion with your staff.

A STEP-BY-STEP APPROACH

In coaching it is important not to try to jump too far forward at each stage of improvement. It is far better to make regular small improvements than to try for one big leap forward. Occasionally big leaps do occur, and when this happens it is usually because the coaching process reveals some major insight for the individual.

Because coaching moves in small steps it does not mean that it is a slow process; on the contrary, by focusing on each area in turn, rapid improvement can occur. If the whole situation were to be tackled in one go then it would be a slow, almost overwhelming battle to improve.

ENCOURAGEMENT AND COMMITMENT – A PARTNERSHIP

Encouragement and commitment go hand in hand.

- Encouragement is something which comes from outside; it is an external stimulant to your efforts.

■ Commitment comes from within. It is your determination to succeed – to do the very best you can. Without your commitment no amount of coaching will help you to improve.

Together these two, encouragement and commitment, can achieve great things. Without encouragement it is difficult to maintain our commitment, especially when things are not progressing as well as we would like.

People need the encouragement of their coach (manager) on every step of the journey, and sometimes it can be hard for you to find encouraging things to say. However, the very least will be for you to encourage your staff for the way they keep trying to improve.

Your staff can also encourage themselves, by telling themselves how well they are doing and taking pride in any and every improvement that they make. This level of self-support is not always easy to summon, but as they receive more encouragement from you it gets easier.

Commitment is an inner drive. Without commitment on both sides there is little point in entering into a coaching agreement with your people. In their endeavours to improve they will face many difficulties, and without commitment these will seem insurmountable. When we are committed we see things differently. We see difficulties as hurdles to jump, not as barriers to success. When such commitment is in evidence it is not a problem for you as coach to be encouraging. But it is very hard to encourage someone who shows no enthusiasm for what is going on.

Encouragement and commitment are a partnership, just as you and your staff are a partnership in striving for improved performance.

COACHING – THE KEY ELEMENTS

There are four key elements in coaching: **encouragement, modelling, step-by-step development** and **support**.

ENCOURAGEMENT

People who are trying to improve performance need constant encouragement to keep trying. There is no advantage in telling someone what they are doing wrong. The important information is *what to do differently* to improve.

See Chapter 8 on giving non-critical feedback.

MODELLING

A critical aspect of coaching is being able to model what you want the person you are coaching to do. Watching something happening and then copying it is a primary learning mechanism that we all have. This has to be done with an understanding of what is happening, so that learners do not misinterpret what they see.

STEP-BY-STEP DEVELOPMENT

Many activities and tasks are quite complex when they are first encountered. Even with experience there are sometimes many things to consider when trying to improve. The good coach will concentrate on one thing at a time, even if it is obvious that several things could be improved. This selection of the element to concentrate on at any one time is an essential feature of good coaching.

Agreeing aims without trying to aim for too much is a crucial part of the coaching cycle.

SUPPORT

We all need support and this is never more true than when we are being asked to try things out as part of the coaching process. We have to know that it is all right if sometimes we do not perform well. We have to be supported when we are learning from our mistakes. Remember, our mistakes should be a basis for learning, not a reason for criticism.

See Chapter 6 on learning from our mistakes.

ACTION LIST – THE COACHING CYCLE

1. Talk to your people about how they might respond to you working as a coach with them.
2. Talk to your staff about areas in which they think they could benefit from your coaching.
3. Make a coaching agreement with each member of your staff.
4. Speak to your boss and endeavour to arrange for the coaching that you think you need.

CHAPTER 12

PERFORMANCE

SUPPORT

KEY LEARNING POINTS
- Understanding what performance support means
- Knowing the elements of performance support
- Understanding the importance of recognition
- Knowing how to motivate people

THE MEANING OF PERFORMANCE SUPPORT

There are many ways that people can be supported in their work, and finding a definition which covers all the possibilities is not easy. Figure 12.1 on page 113 gives my own view of support needed to empower people to be high performers.

Exercise – Performance support

Think about your present job, and prepare a list of the support you need in order to be an exceptional performer. This support might come from your manager, from colleagues and/or your working environment.

Support I need _____

_____

_____

_____

_____

If you have a performance plan select one of your objectives and list the support you need to achieve this specific task.

Task _____

_____

_____

_____

_____

Support I need _____

_____

_____

_____

_____

If this exercise is done for every aspect of your performance plan it becomes clear what you need and expect in order to be a high performer.

THE ELEMENTS OF PERFORMANCE SUPPORT

In Figure 12.1 I have divided support into seven categories. These are purely for the sake of explanation, and you might be able to think of other forms of support that you should provide for your staff which will be relevant to your specific circumstances.

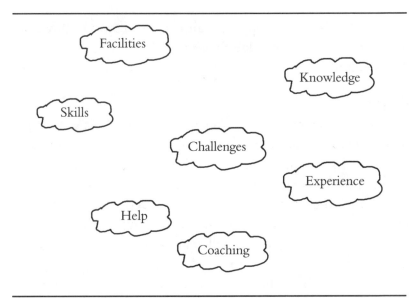

FIGURE 12.1: Categories of support

FACILITIES

When your people are working they may need some basic equipment and resources to do their jobs. I can think of a desk, telephone, computer terminal, and so on. If these facilities are not available when and where they need them, then it becomes impossible for them to be high performers.

Work planning and work organization are two of the least well-done things in the majority of organizations. There seems to be an assumption that people will organize themselves to create the best working arrangements. This is decidedly untrue. Careful, well-designed working practices are essential for any high performing group.

KNOWLEDGE

To perform well, your people will need to know what they are doing. Such an obvious statement and yet many people are promoted into positions without the knowledge, which they then have to acquire. It is called 'learning on the job', or 'being thrown in at the deed end'.

This is particularly true of people who are promoted into a supervisory or management role, and are apparently suddenly endowed with the knowledge of how to supervise or

There is a book in this series, *Sharpen your team's skills in supervision* by Susan Clayton, which addresses this particular issue.

manage. Performance support is aimed at trying to ensure that people have the knowledge they need before or at the time they need it.

SKILLS

Similar to knowledge, people need the proper skills to be high performers. Skill development needs practice and experience, which is best obtained on the job but in a supported way. People new to a particular job will need a lot of support as they begin to gain the experience they need. Being 'left to fend for themselves' is not a constructive approach.

People should receive skill training before they need to use the skills, and to be employed initially in a safe protected environment where they can practise with guidance, and where making mistakes is an accepted part of the learning experience.

CHALLENGES

When work ceases to be challenging it becomes boring, and when work becomes boring it becomes a chore, and when it becomes a chore it becomes poorly executed. It is very hard, if not impossible, for people to perform well in jobs that bore them. Of course our individual levels of boredom are different, and some people will be happy and challenged by routine repetitive work. The key for performance support is to encourage people who are becoming bored to say so and to be given more challenging work.

EXPERIENCE

Experience, as we have seen, is something that is acquired by people being involved in a wide range of activities that test their knowledge and skills to the limit. For each individual, experience will be different because of what we bring to the event in the way of existing knowledge, skill and experience. Providing people with a variety of experience in the work-place is important because it broadens perspective.

See Chapter 5 on the importance of experience.

HELP

Everyone needs help at work, from the chief executive to the newest recruit, but for some reason no one seems to want to admit it. Perhaps asking for help is something that we have been discouraged from doing with expressions such as, 'you should stand on your own two feet', and 'God helps those who help themselves'.

Help should be freely available, and people should be encouraged at all levels to both ask for and to give help to others. Simple 'help sheets' can be prepared for many tasks and activities; these should be readily available.

COACHING

As we have seen in the last chapter, coaching is a continuous and supportive activity that encourages individuals to explore, experiment and try new challenging things. Coaching is a one-to-one guidance system with a more experienced (not necessarily more skilled) person suggesting ways in which a less experienced person might improve. It is one of management's most important activities.

'Welcome, Garry.'

'Thank you.'

'Now this is your first day so I want you to work on the counter serving customers. I know you don't know what to do, or how to do it, but do the best you can.'

Ridiculous, of course, but how often have you heard about someone being promoted and sent out to 'run' their own department equally as poorly supported as Garry? They probably cope, and eventually become good managers. But sometimes when people are 'thrown in at the deep end' they drown.

Exercise – Support needs

Set down under the appropriate headings the support you need in your job *right now* to enable you to become a high performer.

Facilities

_____

_____

_____

Knowledge

_____

_____

_____

Skills

_____

_____

_____

Challenges

_____

_____

_____

Experience

_____

_____

_____

Help

_____

_____

_____

Coaching

_____

_____

_____

THE IMPORTANCE OF RECOGNITION

People like to be 'seen' and appreciated for what they do. It is in fact a fundamental human need and the basis of self-esteem and self-confidence. You will help your people to perform as much by recognizing their achievements as you will by the very best of coaching and support.

Refer to Chapter 8, particularly the section on giving praise.

Recognition makes people feel special. They feel noticed and therefore important in that moment. This feeds messages of acceptance, acknowledgement and respect into their psyche and directly boosts their self-esteem and self-confidence. The effects are powerful motivating factors for the future.

I believe that you should take every opportunity, no matter how small it might seem, to recognize what your people are doing.

MOTIVATING PEOPLE

Motivation is something that we recognize in ourselves when we are keen to do something. Recognizing it and creating it in other people is quite another thing altogether. So what is motivation? Here are some definitions:

> **The act of moving or inducing a person to act in a certain way; a desire, fear, reason, etc. which influences a person's volition.**
> **(Oxford English Dictionary, 1984)**

> **The mental process, function, or instinct that produces and sustains incentive or drive in human and animal behaviour.**
> **(Universal Dictionary, 1994)**

Both these definitions imply that motivation is some kind of force or power that determines the way people act. Neither definition attempts to state where the force comes from. I believe that motivation is the inner fire that burns within everyone. It is there all the time, and is fuelled by all the past experience and conditioning that people have had in their lives. It is stimulated by people's thoughts and by external events that occur in their personal environment. My definition is:

The inner force that makes each person pursue courses of action, both positive and negative, which lead to the satisfaction of some personal desire.

In helping your people to be motivated to high levels of performance you need to be able to help them to tap into their own inner force. Figure 12.2 provides a guide to help you to do this. Complete the framework for each of your staff by discussing each of the sections with them and try to see if you can clearly identify each of the four aspects.

BUILDING BLOCKS
No one can go back and change the past. Whatever has happened to make people who they are has already taken place. What we need is for people to discover their real strengths and skills. These are the building blocks of their future development.

BARRIERS
People allow many things to get in their way. Most of these barriers are self-created based on messages about ourselves. We need to identify all our barriers and systematically tear them down.

BOUNDARIES
We all operate within self-imposed boundaries. We have developed these to help us to survive. If we can see where these are we can start to stretch them as far as we can.

BREATHING SPACE
We all need time and space to review where we are. This space is important to refresh and renew ourselves so plan for it.

FIGURE 12.2: The framework for motivation

In addition to this framework it is helpful to be able to identify what motivates your people to achieve high levels of performance. You will probably find that recognition, respect and reward feature prominently on the agenda.

ACTION LIST – PERFORMANCE SUPPORT

1. Talk to your staff about the support they need in each of the seven areas.
2. Look at your own needs for support and discuss them with your boss.
3. Consider ways in which you can continuously recognize the performance of your staff.
4. Discover what motivates your people to perform by holding a meeting so that they can all contribute to the discussion.

BIBLIOGRAPHY

Bentley, Trevor (1990) *The Business of Training*, McGraw-Hill, Maidenhead.

Bentley, Trevor (1994) *Facilitation*, McGraw-Hill, Maidenhead.

Heider, John (1987) *The Tao of Leadership*, Wildwood House, Aldershot.

Heron, John (1989) *The Facilitator's Handbook*, Kogan Page, London.

Holt, John (1988) *How Children Learn*, Pelican Books, London.

Kolb, David A. (1984) *Experiential Learning*, Prentice-Hall, New Jersey.

Pont, Tony (1991) *Developing Effective Training Skills*, McGraw-Hill, Maidenhead.

Whitmore, John (1992) *Coaching for Performance*, Nicholas Beasley, London.

INDEX

Also from McGraw-Hill

79 / 80 Things You Must Do to be a Great Boss
David Freemantle

'One of my favourite handbooks.'
Kevin Keegan, Manager,
Newcastle United Football Club.
*For managers aiming to get the best out
of their people, this book is a must!*

ISBN: 0 07 709043 8
£12.95

Developing a Learning Culture
Sue Jones

*A highly practical book that should be read by all managers and
trainers who are concerned with implementing change, strategies
and collaborative teamworking."* Management Training.

ISBN: 0 07 707983 3
£19.95

---

101 Ways to Develop Your People Without Really Trying
Peter Honey

*Thousands of ideas on how to fit piggyback learning and
development on the shoulders of normal work activities.*

ISBN: 0 07 709183 3
£16.95

Dealing With People Problems at Work
Steven Palmer and Tim Burton

*'A down-to-earth guide for managers in how to handle a range
of everyday people problems found in most work situations.
This book's practical step-by-step approach will help many who
find their work colleagues a palpable source of job stress."*
Gary Cooper, Manchester School of Management.

ISBN: 0 07 709177 9
£12.95

A Manager's Guide to Self-Development, Third Edition
Mike Pedler

*This working philosophy of
self-development has become the
indispensable guide to helping managers
realise their potential and improve their
abilities and performance.*

ISBN: 0 07 707829 2
£14.95

Developing Managers as Coaches
Frank S. Salisbury

*Based on the view that everyone has a "seed of greatness",
this book will inspire you to leap forward into the crucial concept
of coaching in the business environment.*

ISBN: 0 07 707892 6
19.95

The Power of Personal Influence
Richard Hale

*"A most valuable book which provides a refreshingly practical
approach to improving all aspects of how we influence others."*
Wenche Marshall Foster, Chief Executive, Perrier Group.

ISBN: 0 07 709131 0
£14.95

Vision At Work
John Mitchell

*Highlighting the link between strategy
and the decision-making process, this
book explores how creative leaders can
translate 'vision' into effective 'action'.*

ISBN: 0 07 709085 3
£19.95

Workplace Counselling
Di Kamp

*"Di Kamp is able to describe ways to bring out the best in people.
All that remains now is for the rest of us to implement the ideas."*
Rob Ball, Rover Group Ltd.

ISBN: 0 07 709152 3
£19.95

The Project Manager as Change Agent
J Rodney Turner

*"This text is required reading for all those involved and
interested in the management of change in the 90s."*
Eric Gabriel, Vice-President, Association of Project Managers.

ISBN: 0 07 707741 5
£24.95

The Handbook of Project-Based Management
J Rodney Turner

*A radical re-evaluation of the often overlooked role of the project
manager who has to maximise strategic and successful change.*

ISBN: 0 07 707656 7
£45.00

***Prices are correct at the time of going to press but are subject to change**

Available from all good bookshops

McGraw-Hill Publishing Company
Shoppenhangers Road, Maidenhead, Berkshire, SL6 2QL, England
Tel: ++44 (0) 1628 23431 / Fax: ++44 (0) 1628 35895